Daughter of Labrador

Millicent Blake Loder

Harry Cuff Publications • St. John's • 1989

Acknowledgements

Appreciation is expressed to the Canada Council for publication assistance.

The publisher acknowledges the financial contribution of the Cultural Affairs Division of the Department of Municipal and Provincial Affairs, Government of Newfoundland and Labrador, which has helped make this publication possible.

Canadian Cataloguing in Publication Data

Loder, Millicent Blake, 1915-

    Daughter of Labrador

    ISBN 0-921191-46-4

1. Loder, Millicent Blake, 1915-
2. Nurses — Newfoundland — Labrador — Biography. I. Title.

RT37.L62A3 1989   610.73'092   C89-098681-9

Published by
Harry Cuff Publications Ltd.
94 LeMarchant Road
St. John's, Newfoundland   A1C 2H2

Printed in Canada by
ROBINSON-BLACKMORE PRINTING AND PUBLISHING LIMITED
St. John's, Newfoundland

One : Home and Family • 9

Two : The Mission Schools • 25

Three : North West and "Outside" • 39

Four : Nurse's Training • 53

Five : Back Home • 65

Six : Station Nurse • 83

Seven : Volunteer Midwife • 95

Eight : Back Home to Stay • 111

Nine : Epilogue • 121

I have written this book with all the young people of Labrador in mind, particularly my two grandchildren, Chris and Melynda. You have a proud heritage in this big land that has been handed down to you from your forebears; guard it well for posterity. Keep Labrador free and peaceful, respect its harshness, enjoy its beauty and share it with those who have not been privileged to spend their lifetime in this, our Labrador.

1. Rigolet, my birthplace.

2a. My maternal grandparents, Tom and Anne Oliver.

2b. My parents, John and Jemima Blake.

8

CHAPTER ONE

Home and Family

I always promised my grandchildren, Chris and Melynda, that when I retired and had the time to spare I would tell them all about the "olden times". I began putting my story together on the first day of my retirement, nine years ago. During my retirement I have found, to my delight, that there were many things that I could do to keep myself useful, so this book has taken longer to complete than I thought it might.

I was born in 1915 in Rigolet, a Hudson's Bay Company trading post at the mouth of Hamilton Inlet in Labrador. My parents, John and Jemima Blake, were settlers and I was their fifth child. Of the four who were born before me, only one survived, a six-year-old sister who my grandchildren know as Aunt Margaret.

The "settlers" are one of three main ethnic groups in Labrador. There are the Naskaupi and Montagnais Indians (or Innu), the Eskimos (or Inuit) and the white settlers whose ancestors came from many countries, but mainly from England, Ireland and Scotland. The Indians and Eskimos have lived in Labrador for untold centuries, the settlers came later. There were many reasons why the settlers first came to Labrador; some are said to have run away to escape the press-gangs in Britain, some came as clerks with trading companies and others came because they felt there was wealth to be made in furs. Many of these early settlers married native women, so there are few settler families that do not have Eskimo or Indian blood. Indeed, I am a mixture of all three ethnic groups, as my mother had Eskimo ancestors and my father had some Indian blood. I have been told that my father's family, the Blakes, who are scattered all over Labrador, are descended from four brothers, who came to Labrador from Nova Scotia. Great-grandfather Blake began the family pattern of living in Double Mer for the winter months and in Mulliauk in the summer.

My early childhood was spent partly at Rigolet and partly at a winter

9

home called Burnt Place in Double Mer. Moving about from place to place was necessary to take advantage of the seasons. The Blakes (and my mother's family, the Olivers) made their living by trapping in winter and fishing in summer. This is still practiced in many Labrador communities. The early homes were very simple frame or log dwellings of one or two rooms and a porch. All furniture was homemade; tables, benches for seats, boxes for trunks, bedsteads and always a washstand in the corner of the kitchen. Floors, walls, tables and seats were white and smooth from frequent sandscrubbing. Heat came from iron wood-burning stoves and, since we lived in the bays during the winter, there was no shortage of wood for fuel. All water was carried in buckets from wells, brooks or rivers. Often in winter snow was melted for washing, cooking and cleaning. After sunset the only light was from kerosene lamps, which had to be trimmed, cleaned and filled every day.

Winter houses were usually built in a grove of trees which provided shelter from the cold winds. In my childhood there were about six families wintering at Double Mer. The houses were a mile or more apart, as the base camps for each family's trapline. Outside of each house was a scaffold where fresh meat and fish were kept frozen and safe from the dogs and other animals. Each family had a dog-team and a boat for transportation.

A few years ago, I went up into Double Mer and landed on the beach at Burnt Place, right where our old winter home stood. There in the grass was the frame of the house, parts of an old iron stove and the old wooden table we had used. In the grass I found an old iron boiler with a hole in the bottom. In my mind's eye I could see the old boiler on the stove, filled with snow that was melting for our wash. I took the boiler back and I now use it for a flower pot. The paths that led to the brook, the rabbit snares and the berry grounds have now grown over, but as I walked about the memories came flooding back.

It was usually September when our family moved to the trapping grounds at Double Mer. Ma sat in the boat with all the children around her. She handed out hard tack to keep us quiet while Pa steered the boat and kept an eye out for seals, birds or animals along the beach. Sometimes we would stop while Pa shot a seal or a duck, for we lived mainly off the land. Other times we stopped at Pompey's Head, where Ma's parents lived, for a cup of tea and a break in the trip.

Grandmother and Grandfather Oliver came from Harbour Grace,

in Newfoundland, and settled at Bluff Head, where Grandfather fished. In the fall they moved to Pompey's Head in Double Mer for the trapping season. We always felt a little in awe of Grandfather Oliver but I dearly loved both him and Grandmother. Gran was patient with us when we were learning how to knit or mend or sew sealskin boots. They were both kind, but strict, and they tried to live by the word of God.

In those days people were poor by monetary standards, but they lived in a caring and sharing community, and were rich in family unity. No one went hungry if one person killed a seal. Everyone took turns sitting with the sick, or turned out to haul up or launch a boat, or help put up a house. No payment was offered and none was expected. Ma always told us how good we had it compared to when she was a little girl — the same thing your parents tell you today.

Not far from Bluff Head, at Indian Harbour, there was a hospital run by the International Grenfell Association (IGA), which was open during summer to minister to the needs of the fishermen. In those days many schooners came from Newfoundland to fish for cod all along the Labrador coast. The eldest in her family, Ma was lucky enough to get a job at the hospital as a servant. She was a bright girl and soon learned a great deal about looking after the sick. When she got married and started her own family Ma became a very good midwife and was always the person called on when anyone was sick. We got used to getting up in the mornings and finding her gone. Whenever we asked Pa where she was he would say, "She's gone to find a baby", or "Someone was sick and needed her".

Pa was also the oldest in his family. Grandfather Blake had married a girl by the name of Cluney, from St. John's. Pa, his brothers and sisters were raised in Double Mer and Mulliauk. Pa was a tall, good-looking man and it was easy to see how Ma, whose family lived across the bay, fell in love with him. After they were married Ma and Pa continued the family pattern of moving between a winter home and a summer home.

Moving house, then, is one of the clearest memories that I have of my childhood. When we moved to Double Mer we always arrived at the winter house as early as possible because there was much to do before nightfall. Numerous trips were made back and forth from the beach to the house as we excitedly brought our supplies of food and household goods for Ma to store. While Pa and the boys got wood, splits and shavings and started the fire, the girls would be helping Ma to put things in place and preparing supper. Our meals were always simple, perhaps we would have bread and jam, tea, roast caplin or some other fish or meat. Everyone went to bed early that first night, tired and excited and full of plans for the next day.

We had a lot of work to do to get ready for the winter. The redberries (or partridgeberries) were ripe at that time of year and the whole family joined in to get the winter's supply before the snow came. While we helped Ma gather berries and keep house, Pa would be hunting to add to our supply of meat, or gathering firewood for the months he would be away at the traplines. The biggest chore for Pa was chopping, hauling and piling wood, for he only had one arm. He had to take the dog-team into the woods, beat a path to the trees with his snowshoes on, then cut down the trees and trim off the branches. Then he had to pile them on a wooden komatik and haul the logs home where they had to be sawn, chopped, split and piled. Pa knew he would be on the trapline for several months and he wanted to be sure we had enough wood to last until he returned. He also had to get his traps ready, fill cartridges, mend the dogs' harnesses and prepare bait for the traps. I enjoyed watching and helping him fill the cartridges. The empty shells came ready-made and each was filled with a measure of powder and shot, which Pa made with melted lead. A wad was fitted over the top of the cartridges. There was a vise that screwed onto the tabletop which held the shell in place while it was filled and capped. We enjoyed taking turns turning the handle; it was a fun job. Ma would be busy at the other end of the table, making boots, knitting, sewing or mending warm clothes, and making special duffle and skin sleeves that fitted over Pa's stump.

When I was about two years old Pa had his right arm amputated, just below the elbow, due to tuberculosis of the bone. Since he had been right-handed, he had to learn to use his left hand for all his needs. It must have taken great determination for Pa to learn how to write all over again with his left hand. In the later years that I remember the best, Pa was very efficient with his arm stump. He held his plug tobacco against the stump while he cut the plug with his left hand. With a loop of rope around a wheelbarrow handle he could wheel loads as large as anyone. Pa sculled a boat while others rowed and he could make the chips fly when he cut firewood. He harnessed his dogs using his left hand and his teeth to tie knots and could drive a team as well as any man. It never occurred to me in my childhood that Pa was different from other men. I knew he would come back from his trapline with his fur all skinned and dried, and that he would bring us home fresh meat just like all the other men. As I grew older I realized what a task it must have been for him to cure his fur and what patience and determination he must have had to carry on. My admiration and respect for him still grows, forty years after his death.

Before the boys were old enough to go along, Pa would go into the country alone. One fine morning we would all be out to wave him goodbye. His parting words were always the same, "Look after your Mother".

As soon as Pa went into the country the rest of the family settled in for the winter. Every morning we children awakened to the sound of stove lids clacking as Ma laid the fire for the day. In our small bedroom the boys slept in one bed and the girls in another, all in a tangle of arms and legs. Along the blanket, near our faces, was a line of frost and yet we were warm and comfortable, at least until we got out of bed! When the room warmed a little, Ma called us. We would grab our clothes and run for the stove. Oh, what a flurry of clothes and shouts as we fought for a place near the stove! Often we had to break the ice in the basin before we could dab the sleep out of our eyes, or wait until some water was heated. Almost every morning we had porridge, made either from rolled oats or cornmeal, on which we poured molasses. We always had homemade bread and some butter, which was bought in 5, 10 or 20 pound wooden tubs from the Hudson's Bay Company store at Rigolet. The tubs, when empty, were cleaned and used for water buckets, scrub buckets or berry buckets. Every spring we ran out of butter and then we'd use lard or, sometimes, animal fat for our bread. Bear's fat was really quite good.

After breakfast we did our chores. The boys brought in wood and carried in water. The biggest chore was feeding the dogs. Our sled dogs got one meal, which usually consisted of cooked cornmeal with pieces of blubber and table scraps. One of us would hold the dogs off with a stick while several others would bring out the steaming tub. I often helped with the "boys" chores because I didn't like indoor work. That was all right as long as my older sister was home. She was six years older than I and was very efficient so Ma preferred to have her in the house. I suppose that when I was little I resented Margaret. She had a pretty face with a nice complexion and long, black, curly hair. I had straight hair and was skinny with lots of freckles. Secondly, I had to wear her cast-off clothing and never seemed to get anything new. Margaret seemed to have my mother's attention much more often than I did. However, as I grew up I noticed the same sort of feelings between me and my next sister, Nellie, so I realized that it was not really all Margaret's fault that we didn't get on.

When our work was done what fun we had! In the winter we built snow forts, had snowball fights and made playhouses in the snow under the big spruce trees. We used barrel staves for sliding, or our own small wooden komatiks. The days were never long enough. We had our supper by lamplight, then sat around the stove talking and planning for the next day, learning our Bible verses for Sunday, being taught how to tap boots, knit, sew or make bread, playing string games or singing songs. Before we were ready for it, Ma would be saying, "Get your lunch, say your prayers and go to bed."

Each night, lying warm, cozy and sleepy in bed, the last thing we would see was Ma sitting near the lamp, getting a head start on the next day's work.

Saturdays were bath days. All day the whole family would carry water and melt snow. Every kettle, boiler and saucepan that we owned would be on the stove. In the morning we would scrub the floors, tables and boxes until everything was clean. Then Ma would lay out one of our two shifts of clothes, spotlessly clean, for all the children. We would take turns getting into the tub, which was a wooden barrel cut in half. That night we could stay up later than usual, because our hair had to be dried before we went to bed. Sometimes it wouldn't be quite dry when we went to bed and then it would freeze while we slept.

Sunday was very different from any other day. It was spent very quietly. Some time during the day Ma (or Pa if he was home) would read from the Bible and we would sing hymns, and then we would say the Bible verses we had been learning all week. My brother Bruce, the comedian in the family, was an expert at picking out short verses, his favourite being, "Jesus wept". This made us all laugh, but didn't go over too well with Ma and Pa. It seemed as though Sundays would drag a bit, as we were not allowed to check the snares, ride or play games. Our nearest neighbours were my uncle Willie and his family who lived about a half mile away. Often we would visit them and afterward our cousins would walk part of the way home with us. Soon as we were out of sight of the houses we would have snow fights and "touched-you-last" games. Eventually Sunday would be over and we looked forward to the week ahead.

We looked forward mainly to two things: Pa coming home and Christmas. There was no way of hearing from Pa from the time he left until he came back again. I realize now how hard that must have been for Ma, not knowing how he fared, alone in the bush. Often she stared out through the window at the place on the trail where he had disappeared from view. She used to tell us, as we left the house, "Now, watch for Pa and come and tell me as soon as you see him". Pa would do his best to be home for Christmas.

Other signs of the coming of Christmas were the pies that were kept frozen on the loft in the porch. There would be bakeapple, marshberry, redberry and, sometimes, dried apple pies. There would be at least one goose left on the meat scaffold or in the porch. Even if meat was scarce we would manage to have something for Christmas, but by then there would be no potatoes left. However, Ma could make good things with flour, breadcrumbs and salt pork or beef. In later years you could buy dried onions, which added a lot to our meals.

Around the stove in the evenings we would talk about hanging up our stockings and wondered what Santa would bring. We were always told that if we misbehaved we would only get a stick, so the last month before Christmas we were all well behaved indeed. When I was little I had no idea that other people had things like Christmas trees and decorations; I only found out about that after I left home.

Christmas Eve would come and we would be very excited. The day seemed so long. At last the time would come to hang up our stockings and there would be no trouble getting us to go to bed.

Christmas morning always meant waking up to the smell of apples. We would all get up and make a dash over the frosty floor to our stockings, then back to the warmth of the bed to open them. How excited we were! We would always get a new pair of socks, skin slippers or a pair of mitts. There were homemade wooden toys, or a wooden top made from a spool and there might be a string of beads or a handkerchief. There would be a few common candies and, finally, in the toe of the stocking would be an apple. Those apples really convinced us that there was a Santa Claus. Where else could an apple come from in the Labrador bush? When I got older I learned that the apples were bought with the rest of our fall supplies, wrapped in clothes and put in the middle of a packed box and checked every so often to see if they were keeping. We could make our apples last all Christmas Day and our few candies kept us going until the New Year.

Christmas Day was kept like Sunday, saying prayers, singing hymns and sitting quietly to enjoy our gifts. We felt very fortunate to have our stockings filled. Ma would tell us that there were children so poor that they didn't get anything at all, and that there were children who didn't even know about Christmas. It never occurred to us that there were other people in the world who might think that we were poor.

Pa would usually be home for Christmas, but I can remember once when he got home just before the New Year. We saw him coming and all ran to meet him, taking his sled the last few yards to the house. He had two deer on the sled beside the bundle of furs that he had caught. We helped him carry the deer into the house where they were placed one on each side of the stove, to thaw enough to be skinned and cut up. We were so happy to have Pa home again. He would stay long enough to replenish the woodpile, get his bait ready, have his clothes and boots mended or replaced and then he would go back on the trapline.

My brothers and sisters and I were fortunate indeed, for we had two loving parents and we never felt deprived of anything. We never dreamed of disobeying them, most of the time. Usually, Pa had only to speak to us and we minded, but Ma was softer and we could sometimes get away with some badness. If we were punished and were feeling very upset about it, some word or gesture would let us know we had been forgiven and were loved. Ma told us never to go to bed bearing a grudge against anyone and I have always tried to follow her example, to this day. Ma's sayings and quotations are frequently in my mind and I believe that I profit from them.

Sometimes for Christmas or New Year's we would all go to my grandparents'. Uncle Willie and his family would go along too. Once after we left home a snowstorm came on and it was bitterly cold. By then our family had grown so that we had to have two dog-teams. On this occasion Uncle Bob Mesher was driving one of the teams. I was in the komatik box along with some of my sisters and brothers. On that trip I was the eldest, so I probably had less bedclothes over me. About halfway to Gran's my feet got very cold and I started to cry. It was too cold for me to walk so Uncle Bob would come to the box to slap and wiggle my feet to keep the blood going. After what seemed like a long time I began to feel really warm and cozy. I wanted to go to sleep, but Uncle Bob kept hitting my feet and waking me up. When we got to Gran's she pulled off my boots and stuck my feet in cold water. She then massaged my feet gently until the colour came back. Then I sat on the floor with my feet up under the stove for a long time. I was soon up and around, but my feet were sore for a long time.

It was fairly common for us to get our faces frozen. We were taught to gently rub the area with snow. Today I know that applying something cold is the wrong way to treat frostbite. You must use gradual heat instead of cold; however, there are surprisingly few Labradorians with scarred features due to frostbite, despite the old methods.

16

During the holiday season other people from around Double Mer would come to Gran's and we would all have a wonderful time. The men would have spruce beer and there was always someone who could play the fiddle or the accordion, so there was a dance each night. We children would have a great time, too, playing games, snow fighting, sliding and eating all the special things that had been prepared. Once, when we were playing near the woods, an aunt came out and called us in immediately. When we were safely inside we were told that someone had seen a wolf lurking nearby.

One Christmas at Gran's was a sad time. Grandfather had delivered premature twins to one of our aunts and one had died. (Grandfather often acted as midwife for his married daughters.) The poor baby looked like a small doll in it's wooden box. I think that was the first time I saw a dead person. We had all come to the funeral which was conducted by Grandfather, who also could read quite well and performed most religious ceremonies that could not wait for the minister's visit.

When we went home we settled away for the rest of the winter, for Pa would be gone for another two to three months. Some time during the winter we would, perhaps, get a visit from the doctor and/or the minister. They would come by dog-team visiting all the people who were scattered around the bays and coves of Labrador. Because there was no communication we would not know when these visits would take place. Sometimes a driver from Rigolet might come by and tell us that the doctor or minister was on his way. What a flurry of preparation there would be then! Ma would be busy cooking, cleaning and getting our Sunday clothes ready.

Those visits from the doctor or the minister were big things in our lives. If we were lucky, we saw them once a winter and once in the summer, when they came by boat. We would get our instructions: "Be quiet and mannerly", "Say, 'Yes Sir' and 'No Sir'", "Do not speak when the grown-ups are talking", "Keep your hands, faces and noses clean", "If you're in the house when they are eating, don't stare at them", "Speak when you are spoken to", and so on and so on until the visitors arrived.

Finally, one day a dog-team would be seen coming up the bay. Out would come the spyglass and when the doctor or minister was identified Ma really started to fly. Everyone was dressed up in their Sunday best and the kettle was set to boil. The oldest girl would have been assigned to take care of the baby (there was always a baby, for Ma had a child every two years) which had to be kept quiet so as not to disturb the guests. We didn't eat with the guests. They ate alone, or

17

with Ma and Pa, if Pa was home. It seemed that good things to eat would appear out of the blue. Such important visitors would be served tinned meat, pickles, tinned fruit, milk and sugar and sometimes cheese. We knew that outsiders were used to eating different foods than our usual fare, so we didn't mind not having any. Ma and Pa would sleep on the floor, giving up their bed to the guest. We would put up the driver of the team as well, but the driver was always a Labradorian, who ate with us and could tell us all the news from along the coast. Often someone had died during the winter, perhaps we would learn of a relative who had passed away months before. We were related to almost all the other settler families. The driver would tell us who had good trips to their fur grounds, how the war was going (during the war years, when I was very young) or other news from outside. Those nights we were all up late talking with our guests.

The minister's visits were a busy time, with prayers in all the houses, christening the children born since his last visit. Occasionally, there would be a wedding, though most couples waited until summer when travel was easier and there could be more people for the celebrations. The minister would usually stay only one night, unless the weather got bad. All the while he was there we had prayers, sometimes during the day and always at night. We would all kneel around the wooden benches and boxes. Ma would grow concerned if the weather turned bad. Today, I can understand this concern. She was thinking of the few special foods that were kept for outsiders and she was wondering if there would be anything left if some other guest came along, so perhaps she prayed for a few fine days.

It was always nice to have visitors, but I remember the sense of relief we all felt when the doctor or minister left. It was such a strain to be on your best behaviour that we children sometimes felt like bursting. After the visitors had left, we would always get a lecture from Ma for something we had done or didn't do. The strangers were held up to us as examples of the way we should try to be. I grew up believing that professional people could do no wrong, that they were a different kind of people than we were. The doctor's and minister's visits would often be at the same time, as each serviced the same areas. Once the visits were over we could relax and go back to being just ourselves.

The spring was spent making ready to go back to our summerhouse at Rigolet. Sometimes we went by dogs and komatik and other times by boat. I clearly remember going down quite late one spring. The ice had broken up close to shore and, where the tide was out, there was quite a steep drop from the ballicaters to the rocks below. Rounding one cliff the komatik suddenly sidled off the narrow path. I was terrified but Pa, with his one arm and his superhuman determination, hauled the box back to safety. What a man he was! We always felt safe with him.

After Double Mer, Rigolet seemed a very big place, although it was just a trading post with two or three resident families. There was a Hudson's Bay Company store there and several houses. We headed for one of those houses, which was for the use of the Company servants. For the summer months Pa was a HBC servant. His major duties were as captain of the HBC schooner *Fort Rigolet*, which brought freight and mail from Rigolet to North West River. Later in life he piloted boats of all sizes up through Hamilton Inlet to Goose Bay, when Goose Air Base was being built.

For me, coming back to Rigolet meant being with my special friend, Eva. We were nearly the same age and played together from the time we were little, for hours and hours every summer. We had a playhouse, a clearing among the trees. Our table was a big flat rock and our dishes and cooking gear were pieces of broken dishes. For dolls we had sticks that we wrapped in leaves or a bit of cloth that we had found and washed. We had so much to do that the days were never long enough.

Our childhood was short for, as soon as possible, children were taught to do the household and outdoor chores, and we had to take responsibility for looking after younger brothers and sisters. In those days there was no birth control and none was wanted, since a big family was seen as usual and necessary, so there were always babies. Eva and I loved babies.

Summer was very exciting. The fishermen were always coming and going from the Hudson's Bay post at Rigolet. The HBC provided a kitchen where the comers and goers could get their lunches and sometimes our family would be the ones who stayed in the kitchen and looked after them. I don't believe that Ma was paid for the work; I guess it came with the privilege of staying in a Company house. There were times when people were weather-bound for several days, there always seemed to be people sleeping on our floor. If you got up in the night you had to step over sleeping bodies.

In those days most people had only rowboats for getting about. You knew who was coming when they were a long way off, because of the direction they were coming from, the colour of the boat and the action of the rowers. Some people from 'up the bay' (meaning Lake Melville and particularly North West River) had motorboats. They seemed to be better off, they dressed better and seemed to have more supplies than we did. Perhaps it was the influence of the International Grenfell Association, which had a hospital in North West River and provided some jobs, promoted education and encouraged development in other ways.

Another great thing in the summer was the coming of the mail boat, about once a month. This was a steamer that came from St. John's, Newfoundland, bringing mail and goods to all the small places along the Labrador coast. We would have some idea of when the steamer was coming and we would watch for the smoke rising over Lester's Point. As soon as we saw the smoke, we would start shouting and running to all the houses to let them know the *Kyle* was coming. In our eyes the *Kyle* was a grand ocean liner. If you could get aboard and get a peep in the dining salon, or the smokeroom, and you saw some of the people who were travelling, well, your summer was made and you had something to talk about for a long time. Some of the tourists came ashore and would go around among the houses. Sometimes we would see them peeking into our homes to see what we had and how we lived. We all knew this was very rude. Sometimes they would ask if you had any fur, skin boots or grass work to sell. Whenever this happened, we were warned not to mention it to anyone. If it got to the ears of the HBC boss it might cause trouble for Pa. The Hudson's Bay Company supplied the trappers and in return they were supposed to get all the fur. However, the tourists knew that they could get much better prices from the trappers, who kept a few items to sell for cash.

There was no pier, so the *Kyle* anchored a long way off from shore. The freight would be towed ashore in a scow. We watched the unloading and could sometimes tell from the boxes what had come, so we could run home and tell Ma. All goods came in wooden boxes, puncheons, barrels and tubs. As things were opened in the store we watched for common candy. Sometimes, if you did a little job in the store, you would be paid with a few candies; for us that was payment enough. In the store there was a hatch through which the empty boxes were dropped. Since the buildings were built up on shores, and wooden walkways connected all the buildings, you could crawl underneath the store. When we saw an empty candy box being dropped we would go down and get it and eat the crumbs. Sometimes the pieces would be quite big. If anyone saw us we would say that we were getting boxes to make splits and shavings, which was often true, since nothing was ever wasted.

Most utensils around the house were made by the men of the

20

household. Barrels made good washtubs and dogs' feed tubs. Butter tubs became scrub buckets, water buckets and berry containers. Boxes made dressers, storage bins and so on, according to their sizes. Many houses were made from bits and pieces of boxes for, while forests grew all around, there were no sawmills and all lumber was shipped in from outside or sawn by hand.

Sometimes one of us would get a trip with Pa on the *Fort Rigolet*. Once Eva and I went on the first trip of the summer and got caught in the ice for a while. A polar bear was around the area, but we had no need to fear with men and guns on board. This was my first trip to North West River, which lies at the head of Hamilton Inlet. I was going to visit uncle Mark Blake. Although Pa told us about Indians, or Mountaineers as he called them, I had never seen one before, as most of the people I knew were a mixture of settler and Eskimo. Pa said he got along well with the Mountaineers in the bush, even though they couldn't speak each other's language. He said they drank tea together and exchanged small furs for tea and tobacco. When we arrived at North West River I saw Indian people for myself. I was a little scared, as all children are when they see someone different.

The Indians came to North West River each summer and put up their tents along the grassy slopes, across the river from the hospital. In the fall they would get their supplies, load their canoes and go back up the beautiful Grand River. It was a pretty sight, in early summer, to look out in the evening and see all these canoes coming downriver loaded with families and furs, and later to see their fires as they put up their tents. I soon got used to the Indian people, who were a friendly, good-looking, dark-complexioned people. They wore beautiful moccasins, jackets and headbands which the women had made. The women wore their hair in a style that was both neat and practical. They had rolls of hair bound on each side of their heads. They put needles in these rolls, much the same as we do in pin-cushions. The women's moccasins were usually beaded or worked with silk. The Indians were kind and friendly to us, and I enjoyed playing with the children. I loved the little babies. They would be placed on baby boards and set outside the tents on fine days.

North West River was a beautiful place with warm sandy beaches, while in Rigolet the beaches were mostly rock and, because we were open to the ocean, the water was much colder. On my first visit I knew that North West River was where I most wanted to live.

So the summers and winters sped by. We were happy, content and secure in our family circle. We went to bed each night with eager anticipation of the next day. We knew little of the world outside of Labrador. We were often told that when we got old enough we would be going to school, and there we would learn about the rest of the world. We were told that we were to take every opportunity to better ourselves. I know now that if we had followed our parents' lifestyle we could always walk with pride, for the people of Labrador were people who had come to grips with the everyday problems of making a living in a virgin country, and who brought up their children with the knowledge of and respect for their land. As I grew older, I came to appreciate more and more the beauty and wealth of the land where I was fortunate enough to be born.

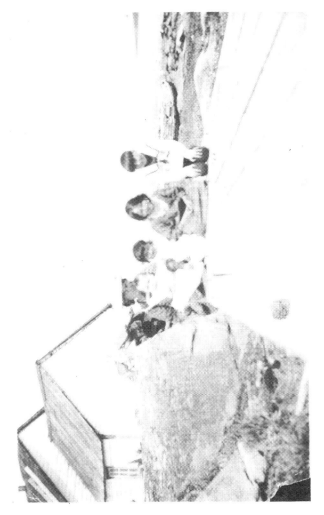

3. My brothers and sisters in front of the HBC house in Rigolet. I am second from right.

4. *The mission school at Muddy Bay. Photo courtesy Frances (Conrow) Pye and* Them Days.

CHAPTER TWO

The Mission Schools

I know that I have already mentioned the International Grenfell Association, but since it has played such a big part in my life, perhaps I should say a few more words about the IGA at this point in my story.

In the year 1892 a young English doctor named Wilfred Grenfell came to Newfoundland to care for the Newfoundland fishermen who, in those days, came to the teeming fishing grounds off Labrador to load their schooners once or twice during the summer. As there were no hospitals or nursing stations, it was necessary to have a visiting doctor. Dr. Grenfell was the son of a Protestant minister and a friend of the great evangelist Moody. It was not surprising, then, that Grenfell was a religious man himself and was influenced by Moody to believe that religion was expressed through service to mankind. As he journeyed along the coasts of Newfoundland and Labrador, Dr. Grenfell was appalled by what he called "abject poverty" among the people. There were no schools and no medical services of any kind. People looked after each other, as best they could, using home remedies. Many endured much suffering. Tuberculosis was rampant. The birthrate and infant death rate were high. The only stores were the HBC stores which were sparsely scattered along the coast and carried only the bare necessities. Dr. Grenfell saw the great need of these people and decided to dedicate his life to doing something about it.

Grenfell built his first small hospital at Battle Harbour in 1893. Later that same year he started a second hospital at Indian Harbour. Both locations were good fishing areas with safe harbours so the schooners gathered there. That winter Dr. Grenfell established a pattern that was to last many years. He went on speaking tours throughout Canada, the United States and England, telling of the plight of the Labrador people. He received many donations from organizations and private citizens to pay doctors' salaries and to build hospitals through the International Grenfell Association. Eventually, the IGA established a network of hospitals, nursing stations and schools all over the northern part of Newfoundland and the Labrador coast. Wherever a station, hospital or school was built, a different way of life came to the people of that area. The people learned to value the new way of life while still retaining their pride in the old ways. One wonders what life would be like in Labrador today had it not been for Dr. Grenfell. The government of Newfoundland had taken little interest in this part of the country until IGA showed the way, and even today the Grenfell Regional Health Service has a strong voice in seeking benefits for the people of Labrador.

In the evenings, when our family gathered around the warm stove in Double Mer, we would often talk about the great things we would do when we grew up. I always told my brothers and sisters that I was going to "find babies" when I grew up. (Ma told us, when we were little, that she found the babies she brought to people in rotten stumps, but my sisters and I searched in all the stumps we could find without seeing one baby.) My brothers were going to be hunters, trappers or soldiers. Ma would always speak up and tell us that whatever we were going to be, we had to go to school to learn to read and write, so that we could make something of ourselves.

I started school when I was about eight in a small one-room school at Rigolet, where each year a young teacher came from Newfoundland, supplied by the Church of England. At one end of the building there was a kitchen and a bedroom, built especially for the teacher. Older boys were responsible for lighting the wood stove each day before school started, and for keeping it going all day. Wood and water for the school were supplied by the village people. The first year I went to school only for the summer months, but the next year the school was completed and classes were held all winter at the usual time. I can recall learning to make letters and figures. We wrote on a slate with a slate pencil that scratched and set your teeth on edge. When fall came, and the rest of the family went to Double Mer and our winter home, I was left behind with neighbours so that I could attend school full time. Eva and I became competitors in school. At the end of that first year I was heartbroken when Eva beat me by a few marks for first place in our grade. At home I threw my skipping rope (second prize) out the door and lying down on the grass, I sobbed my heart out. When I stopped crying, Ma told me how proud she was of the marks I had brought home. During the summer my disappointment faded and I was happy to learn that my parents had made arrangements for me to attend the Boarding School at Muddy Bay, near Cartwright, which was owned and operated by the Grenfell Mission. Ma was busy the last few weeks that summer, making my older sister's clothes over to fit me. She made skin boots and duffles for the winter and helped me to knit long woolen socks. All the while she told me to be a good girl, to be respectful to my elders and to let the family know how I was getting on.

Early in September the IGA hospital boat, *Strathcona* steamed into Rigolet harbour and I was rowed aboard after saying good-bye to the rest of the family, dressed in my Sunday best, ten years old and leaving my family behind. I was the only child on board so I was placed in the dispensary of the boat and told not to touch anything. The half door was barred for safety, and I was alone. As the houses of Rigolet faded in the distance, I became homesick and stood peeping above the door, crying and miserable. Finally Dr. Grenfell himself came in and sat me on his knee. He started leafing through a magazine, telling me about the things and places pictured there. He came to one picture of a very grand lady. He told me that if I was a good girl, worked hard and got a good education I would one day be a lady. This was the one time in my life that I spoke to Dr. Grenfell face-to-face, but I always remembered his kindness when he would come to visit the schools in later years. Like most of the children who knew Dr. Grenfell, I loved him dearly.

When we arrived at Muddy Bay, the school looked monstrous to me. The staff and children of the school came down on the wharf to greet us. I was taken to the school and was handed over to the Head Mistress. She looked at me, then called one of the working girls over and said, "Take her upstairs and show her where she is going to sleep. Check her head, give her a bath and put some decent clothes on her". I was heartbroken. I was being treated like I imagined poor children were, and I knew that my mother had given me the best she could.

This being my first time away from home, I suffered severe homesickness for a long time at Muddy Bay school. Gradually, I made friends with the other children, but I still found school life very different from home. There were so many rules and regulations to get used to. You were not allowed to go into the staff room. You had to ask permission to go out and to come in. Eat everything on your plate. Make your bed before leaving your room. Button the clothes of the younger children. Take your cod oil without fussing. There seemed no end to the list of what you should and shouldn't do.

I soon learned to adjust. My happiest hours were spent in the library.

I could read quite well by then and soon got hooked on books. I often hid away in the small library, behind a chair or in a dark corner, and read everything I could lay my hands on. One time I was caught hiding away in the library and wasn't allowed to have a book for a whole week. This was real punishment for me.

We all had our chores to do; some peeled potatoes (when there were any), others swept and scrubbed the floors, or cleaned and trimmed the lamps. I played with and minded the little ones, because I was ten and used to caring for my brothers and sisters. It was considered a great privilege to be allowed to dust and tidy the staff rooms, or to mend the teachers' clothing, darn their socks and perhaps to iron some of their things. The teachers had such nice things; clothes with lace on them, pretty beads, flowered hand mirrors — real treasures. Sunday was a special day at the school. There was no studying, so we spent the day reading, playing and having services. Each pupil recited the Bible text set for that week. For an extra special treat each Sunday, as we filed out of the dining room after supper, we were given a candy.

During the winter our teacher told us that someone had offered a five-dollar gold piece for the boy and girl who got the highest marks in school. I intended to work hard for such a fortune. That winter flew by and finally we had our exams. When our grades were handed out, I was very proud to find out that I had won the five-dollar gold piece for the girls. John Heard was just as proud to win the boys' prize. Our money was locked in the school for the next year and I got ready to return home for the summer. A short trip on the *Kyle* dropped me at Rigolet. Oh, it was good to be home to a loving family!

When I returned to Muddy Bay for my second year at school my brother Stanley and my sister Nellie accompanied me. They too suffered the pain of homesickness, but now I was an old hand at school and, hopefully, I made things easier for them. I think it was early that fall that there was an outbreak of scarlet fever. Those of us who were affected were all isolated in the same room, and once the fever stage was over what fun we had! That year there was a nurse with us. She must have had her hands full. As soon as her back was turned, we were out of bed and throwing things out the window to others, who were gathered below our window when they weren't in class. They, in turn, would try to throw things to us until we got caught and were forced to stop.

Long before Christmas we were all well and back into the classroom in time for the excitement that precedes the visit of Santa Claus.

28

Although I can remember the Christmases at home extremely well, I cannot recall the details of my two Christmasses at Muddy Bay. I do remember the tree and the decorations that I saw for the first time, and the holiday time when we were free to be out sliding and playing. Best of all, there was plenty of time for reading.

One cold Sunday in February we were all in the dining room eating supper and sneaking looks at the candy we would get as we filed out of the room. Suddenly one of the servants came in and spoke to the Mistress, who always stood and watched us while we ate. She told us to get up and quietly go out the door, go straight down the hall and out of the front door. We did as we were told, although most of us felt like grabbing our candy as we walked past. As we passed the stairway, there was smoke coming down and we could hear a fire crackling. Outside the door someone told us to go down on the harbour and go to Mr. Birdseye's cottage where we were to wait (the Birdseye frozen food company had several buildings at Muddy Bay). We could see the school burning from the window. I had taken Stanley and Nellie with me, and we all tried to look after the little ones. It was very cold, as we were unable to grab our coats or parkas in the rush to get out. Soon we were wrapped in blankets and on our way to Cartwright. It was only a short distance, but the cold was bitter. The manager of the HBC store at Cartwright opened the store, made a hot fire and had hot cocoa and biscuits ready for us when we arrived. Soon the kind people of Cartwright came and took us into their homes where they fed, comforted and clothed us as best they could.

By the next morning we all knew that our school had burned to the ground. One little girl barely escaped. A teacher managed to get her out through a window and to those standing below, then the teacher jumped from the porch and injured his knee. It is tragic to note that this same girl lost her life when a newer and safer dormitory, built at Cartwright, was destroyed by fire some years later.

The laundry building, near the school, was left undamaged, so it was decided that the six children who were taking grade six would stay and finish the year. The laundry was turned into a school room and the bunkhouse, which had been used by Birdseye's people, was done up to give us a place to stay. The HBC gave us some ledgers for scribblers, some pencils and sent wooden crates to be used as desks. As soon as we went back to Muddy Bay, I went poking through the ashes of the school to see if I could find my five-dollar gold piece. I never did.

The people along the coast gradually learned of the fire and came to get their children. When Pa came to get Stanley and Nellie, I didn't mind staying because by this time I loved going to school, and I wanted to get my grade six. Pa said if I got my grade six perhaps I could go to St. Anthony, in Newfoundland, and continue in school as high as grade nine.

Coming home on the *Kyle* that summer, I felt that I was very lucky. I knew I would be going to St. Anthony in the fall, where I would get my final three grades. I also knew that my desire to find babies and care for the sick and injured, as Ma always did, meant becoming a nurse. I didn't yet know how I could become one, or indeed very much about what nurses did, but I was determined that I would be a nurse one day.

Whatever else I did at Muddy Bay, I learned a lot from my private reading. I read everything, good and bad, and made up my own pronunciations and meanings for words I didn't know. There may have been a dictionary around but I was not aware of one, nor had I been taught how to use one. Later I found that I had to relearn a lot of words and meanings; I also knew that much knowledge had been lost to me by reading without guidance. Apart from school, I learned about life in general at Muddy Bay. I learned that some of the people we were taught to regard as models had feet of clay. The staff was good to us, but always let us know that we were not their equals. The staff came from abroad and felt themselves to be missionaries, trying to bring a bit of England to the Labrador wild. In the same building, they ate apart from us, had different food and better living quarters. I'll bet there were some children, especially the boys, who had never seen the staff quarters. It was off limits. Worst of all was when you had been spanked, or otherwise punished, there was no one to put their arms around you to comfort you and let you know you had been forgiven. One of the worse punishments was having to go without your meal, because you were young, active and always hungry. It is sad to note that, when the school burned down, the fire had been set by a boy who had been sent to his room and was to have no supper. No matter what else happened there, I clearly remembered the greeting of the Head Mistress on my first day at Muddy Bay. For the rest of my time in the school I tried to keep out of her way, for I felt she didn't like me. In later years I have always tried to remember that children are very sensitive and intelligent people, and they must always be spoken to and treated with care and kindness. There were many good times to remember of my two years at Muddy Bay, and I left with some sadness, but I was full of joy to be going home.

Back at home in Rigolet that summer seemed especially short. Ma was busy sewing and knitting and, at last, I was getting some new things of my own because my older sister had gone to work for the IGA. When the minister and doctor visited that summer I felt very grand in my new cotton print. Ma was extra busy that summer for, in addition to my going to St. Anthony, some of my younger brothers and sisters were going to go to boarding school at North West River. We all helped as much as we could. Since Margaret was gone, it was my luck to have to do housework. I didn't mind the cleaning and minding the little ones, but I hated the cooking. There was little time for reading and in any case the only books we had were a Bible and copies of *The Family Herald* and *Star Weekly*, worn out from being passed from hand to hand.

I daydreamed all summer about going away. This time I was going farther than before and would not be able to get home until the boats started in the summer. Sometimes I wondered what I would do if Ma or one of the family got sick. My friend Eva was going to St. Anthony too, and we spent all our free time talking about the coming year. I got many lectures from Ma about how to behave and how to speak to people. I was warned over and over to say my prayers, to go to church and to write home by every boat.

Excitement mounted as the summer wore on. The last week I packed and repacked my small wooden box: skin boots, wrapped in paper in the bottom so they wouldn't make the other things smell, new knitted socks, new dickie, two changes of clothing and my Sunday clothes. At last the day came when the *Kyle*'s smoke rose over Lester's Point. How excited I was, and yet I felt like crying. The family came down to the wharf to see me off. Pa stood in the little boat that took us out to the *Kyle*. I said good-bye to him as I transferred to the big boat. Pa's last words were, "Be a good girl".

Eva and I were used to the people on the *Kyle* for we had been going back and forth to school for two years. Mr. Sparrow, the Purser, was a special friend, who was always good to me. There also was the Chief Steward, Ben Penney. Over the years those two men looked after us and gave us some sound advice. The whole crew was good to us and they took pains to see that we were safe. It must have been a relief to our parents that there were such people on the coastal boat. I was never homesick on the *Kyle*.

We were lucky enough to have bunks on our trip to St. Anthony. Very often fishermen and their families, going home to Newfoundland after the fishing season, had to travel on deck or down in the hold of the ship. They would have little stoves and we could watch them having their meals. The smells were so good: cabbage, salt beef and fish. Many evenings there would be singing and someone playing the accordion. Occasionally there would be a dance on deck. The coastal boat called at every harbour where the Newfoundlanders were fishing. Some of the "stationers" came out to the *Kyle* to load supplies, others were going south to their home ports. Others came on board to see the doctor or medical student, who travelled on the boat all summer to care for the needs of the fishermen and livyers. (The "livyers" were the people who "lived here", on the coast of Labrador, all year.)

Time passed pleasantly on the boat as long as you kept your place and didn't bother the first-class passengers or go on the bridge. Many times the cook would hand us a piece of pie or cake. I thought it was grand to travel on the *Kyle*. Someone made your bed, you were waited on at the table and the meals were excellent. You had a choice of meat or fish, and, as the Steward always asked, 'Pudding or pie?' Sometimes the tourists would talk to us even though we were only children. Then, before you were ready for it, it was the end of the journey.

I can recall quite clearly my first sight of St. Anthony. There was fog around and for some time we had been hearing a foghorn, the first one I had ever heard. As we rounded the Cape, St. Anthony was spread out around us. There were many houses around the harbour and I saw two churches, one on each side of the harbour. We tied up at a wharf, the size of which I had never seen before. Up from the wharf were several large buildings that belonged to the IGA. There was a large shed and farther up, enclosed by fences, was a large yellow box-like building. This was the orphanage, where we were to live. Five Labrador girls and a number of boys had come to attend school that year.

We were met and warmly welcomed by a jolly, smiling, motherly sort of lady. This was Miss Karpik, the Head Mistress. Her greeting convinced me from the first that this school would be more to my liking than Muddy Bay. Miss Karpik took us around to our room. This was called the Labrador Girls' Room. Other children were everywhere in the halls and in the dining room. Some had been there for years, while others were newcomers as we were. The dining room had lots of tables and when we all filed in they were all full. It was like a big family. Miss Karpik and her helpers sat at the table with us, quite a change from Muddy Bay. Miss Karpik told us all about the rules and regulations. She told us that she would be glad to help us out with anything at any time. I loved her from the first. That night we were allowed to go out for a little while. There were swings at the front of the building, real swings with chains and seats. We spent the evening swinging up high and getting a good look all around St. Anthony. I told Eva I was going to like it here. After we got in bed we chatted about the place, the Head Mistress and expectations for the future. We fell asleep happy.

The next morning, on the way to school, I took a good look at the buildings. Everything was clean and neat. There were Bible verses on some of the buildings, which made me feel more at home than anything else. I had heard those verses many times. There was a building next to the hospital where patients who were not hospitalized stayed. On the building, in big black letters, was "Faith, hope and love abide and the greatest of these is love". On the school was "All thy children shall be taught of the Lord and great shall be the peace of thy children".

School at St. Anthony was an enchantment from that day. There were four classrooms with a teacher in each room. Each room had several grades. My teacher was Miss Frances Byers, an American. I would have done anything to please her and I believe most of her class would have done the same. After all these years I remember her with love and appreciation. She put us on the right track to gaining knowledge and understanding, to enjoy competition and success and how to accept defeat and profit from it. For the first time I felt that I could relate to an "outsider" as a friend. Shortly after I arrived, Miss Byers asked me if I would help her clean her room and do up her clothes on Saturdays. I was very flattered. The first Saturday I cleaned, ironed and sewed some things for her, and I was surprised when she gave me twenty-five cents. I had my own spending money! While I stitched or darned, Miss Byers told me about other countries and other people. Soon I began to realize how small my world was.

Perhaps because I was older, I felt that I had a lot of freedom at St. Anthony. On Sundays we were free to go out after dinner and do what we liked, as long as we were back by mealtime. Sometimes you might be asked to have a meal by some of the townspeople and permission was always given. Quite often we walked across the harbour or up the Bight, and we would be invited into the homes. We would be given bread and molasses or jam, and sometimes a cup of tea or other tidbits. Some of the dearest friends I have today are people that I met at St. Anthony.

In my second year at St. Anthony, I contracted typhoid fever. There were quite a number of cases. It was late fall and I remember Miss Karpik sponging me down and getting me to drink. I really didn't know how ill I was so it didn't worry me at all. The last boat of the season was expected shortly on its last trip north, so one evening Miss Karpik got me to dictate a letter to my mother. That was one of the most kind and thoughtful acts that had ever been done for me. I shall never forget it. One night, not long after I got ill, two men came and carried me to the hospital on a stretcher. That was the first time I had ever been in a hospital. I took little notice of anything for the first few days, but as I began to feel better I became interested in the activities of the hospital. I found that hospitals have a smell of their own, a good clean smell. Everything was spotless, the staff was kind and pleasant and everyone was always busy with the patients. Every day the doctors came around and told the nurses what to do. The aides brought in meal trays and fed you until you got strong enough to feed yourself. They were so good and patient I would force things down even when it nearly gagged me, just to please them.

One night I was wakeful and watched an aide who was sitting outside the door of a very ill patient across the hall from me. It was very frightening. The electricity was turned off at ten and the patients were then cared for by lamplight. The lamplight was on the face of the aide, and I could sense the worry and concern there. All the while the sound of laboured breathing came from the room. Occasionally the Nurse would come and speak to her, glancing at the patient and go on her way. When the breathing stopped it got so very quiet. I sensed that the patient had died. I got very little sleep the rest of the night. In the morning that same Aide brought us our breakfast with her usual bright and cheerful "Good Morning". I was the only one who knew what a hard night she had.

I was in the hospital for a long time, typhoid fever being a very debilitating condition. By the time I left I knew for sure that some day I would be a Registered Nurse.

I had lost a lot of school and worried that I would have to repeat the year. For the next few months I tried very hard to catch up. Miss Byers helped me a great deal on our Saturdays together. After I had returned to Rigolet that summer I received a letter from her saying that I had passed my grade with honours and that she was very proud of me.

The last year at St. Anthony flew by. There were new teachers to get used to and always new things to do. That year there were two teachers named Morris, one an American and the other from Newfoundland. We called them Miss American Morris and Miss Newfoundland Morris to distinguish them when speaking of them. The teachers were willing to put in much extra time with us in the evenings, practising for plays, singing or playing games.

In the Labrador Girls' room that last year, we talked ourselves to sleep most nights after "lights out". We talked mostly of what we were going to do once we finished school. One girl, like me, wanted to be a nurse. Two others were going to be teachers. I expected it would take years before I would be head nurse at the little hospital at North West River, but by this time this was my main ambition.

I don't recall being homesick at St. Anthony. Our days were full and there were so many new things to get used to. It was at St. Anthony that I saw electric lights for the first time. I saw the inside of a hospital. I saw nurses at work, learned what an X-ray was and I visited the dentist. I began to understand why outside people were so different, for the world outside that I was being taught about was very different from Double Mer and the things and ideas that the Grenfell Mission had brought to St. Anthony were the wonders of the world compared to Rigolet.

5b. Our beloved Miss Karpik and residents of the orphanage at St. Anthony.

5a. Loading up the dogteam outside a winter house in Mulliauk.

6. Children at the St. Anthony orpharge. I am marked with an X, right.

7. *The hospital at North West River, as it was when I worked there as a maid.*

CHAPTER THREE

North West and "Outside"

In my dreams at the Labrador Girls' Room in St. Anthony I pictured myself dressed in white and working as the nurse in charge of the North West River hospital. I dreamed that I would pattern myself after Miss Carlson, the head nurse at the St. Anthony hospital. She was Swedish born, trained in the United States and had been in St. Anthony for many years. Miss Carlson was a very dignified, organized and fair person. I watched her admiringly as she went among the staff and patients. I saw how she handled them and saw the respect they gave her.

When I finished my grade nine my parents wondered what could be done with me. I was considered old enough to work, but there was little for girls to do in those days. I felt that I had learned enough at St. Anthony to be of great help to my mother and be able to take over for her when she went to deliver a baby or look after someone sick, but Ma knew of my ambition and tried to encourage it as best she could. Once again she put her pride in her pocket and approached Dr. Harry Paddon at North West River to see if there was a job I could do with the IGA. Later that summer I got word that I could come to North West River to work as a servant girl in the hospital. I was overjoyed. Ma and I worked to get me ready. It was 1929; I was fourteen.

As I sailed up beautiful Hamilton Inlet toward North West River and my first job, I dreamed of what might come of this position. I hoped to earn enough to be able to go on to school and later become a nurse. I was also looking forward to seeing my older sister, who had married and settled in North West River, and to seeing the people who came down for the salmon fishing every season. I felt grown-up and confident that I would see my dream come true.

Arriving at the hospital, the girls who worked there got me settled away and told me what to expect in the morning. I stayed with two other girls in one room. It was good to have their company and listen to their advice about how to handle the work, what the staff was like and how to please them.

Our days began early. We got up at five-thirty or six o'clock to start the fires in the kitchens. There were two small kitchens; one for the staff and one for the use of patients. That first month I was ward maid. In my patients' little kitchen I lit the fire, cooked their breakfasts, gave them their meals, helped to feed those who could not feed themselves, washed the dishes and cleaned the kitchen. Following breakfast, the patients had to be washed and their beds made. The two small wards, one tiny operating room, the linen closet and dispensary had to be all cleaned, tidied and dusted. There was no electricity and no running water. Oil lamps had to be cleaned, filled and trimmed. Slop pails had to be emptied, washed and returned to the rooms. Then we did whatever jobs the nurses had for us. Soon it was time for dinner, feeding the patients, doing dishes and getting our own meals. Each day we had our additional duties. Mondays were wash days. We did the washing for all the staff, patients and ourselves in wash tubs on wash boards. The clothing was spread outside to dry in the sun and wind, both summer and winter. Tuesdays we ironed and mended. All girls worked together at these jobs. At least twice a week we did all the floors on our hands and knees with scrubbing brushes. Most nights after supper, and after the patients were settled away, we prepared for the next day. In the basement we would have such fun and laughter as we sang and joked, while feathers flew, as we picked partridges for the next day's meals. Even in the hospital, we lived mainly off the land. Many times when we finished preparing for the next day it was time for bed.

We all got one half-day off a week, which we looked forward to. It began after we had fed the patients and staff, cleaned up the dinner dishes and prepared the supper. It was a very short half-day sometimes, but we enjoyed it. Sometimes we went snowshoeing. Sometimes we took a twenty-two and went to look for partridges. There was always a place where we could fish through the ice. I spent a lot of time with my sister. There were times, too, when the hospital staff would take a whole day and go up in the lake smelting. In the fall there would be a day when we would all go gathering berries, preparing for winter.

My starting salary at the hospital was fifty cents a month. How I looked forward to my first payday! At that time the Grenfell Mission was financed entirely by donations. I suppose that was why our wages were so low. I do remember occasionally we would all be called together by Dr. Paddon; he would tell us that the Mission was having a hard time and ask if we would be willing to work a month or two without wages. Of course we always did. We were still getting free meals and a bed to sleep in. As far as I was concerned I was learning something about my trade.

We did not wear uniforms, but supplied our own clothing. Donations of clothes were sent to the Mission and we were able to buy things very cheaply. Although I believe the donations were meant to be given free to the people of Labrador, we always paid a little for whatever we got. If people didn't have any money, they traded meat, berries, deer-skin slippers, or some such thing to the IGA for clothes. You could get a dress for twenty-five cents, which would mean that I could buy a dress and still have twenty-five cents left from my month's wages. A coat cost more than fifty cents, but you could get one if you owed some of your next month's wages. I had been taught at home that you should always pay for what you got and leave charity for poor people.

The three of us took turns at doing the cooking, cleaning the staff quarters and working as ward maids. In my second month at North West River it was my turn as cook. For me, cooking was a month to endure. Patients and servants ate the same food, while doctors, nurses, teachers and other outsiders had specially cooked foods, for they were not used to our kind of cooking.

The first time it came my turn to do a month as staff girl, I was very excited. I hadn't been in the staff quarters, except in the living room once or twice. Remembering the pretty things the teachers at Muddy Bay had, I was looking forward to seeing what the outsiders had at North West River. First thing I did every morning was to take a jug of warm water to the rooms of the doctor, nurses, teachers and other outsiders and awakened them. While they were dressing, I was preparing their breakfast. The cook would see to it that the coals were just right for making toast, which was made at the last minute so that it would be hot. The table had to be set just so. When the staff assembled and were seated at the table, a little bell would summon the staff girl in with breakfast. After breakfast all the bedrooms had to be done — beds made, lamps trimmed and cleaned, everything dusted and tidied and the slop pails emptied and cleaned. I hated this part of the job. I didn't mind doing for sick people, but I promised myself that when I got to be a nurse I would look after my own things. In addition to the normal daily duties there was one other job for the staff girl, making butter balls. There were two little wooden paddles with grooves in them and a pattern on one side. You dipped the paddles in ice water and placed a blob of butter on them, then rolled it around to form little balls with a pattern on them. I bit my tongue to keep from asking what difference it made. For supper the staff would all dress and the staff girl would have to wear a black dress with a frilly apron and a little white headdress. You lighted the lamps and built a fire so that everything would be warm and ready for supper. After the dishes were done and other chores taken care of, you had to turn down the staff beds and make sure there was water in their jugs. Sometimes, if it was really cold, a little kerosene stove was lit and moved from room to room to take the chill off the air.

For four years I went from one job to the other and back again. I enjoyed most of my work and endured the things I did not like, because I knew that some day I would get to be a nurse. I learned a lot and grew to think of North West River as the place I loved best. I became even more determined to come back when I eventually got through my training.

There is no question that I was learning some of the things I would need to know to be a nurse. I clearly remember the first delivery I helped with. I remember the dog-team that brought a badly burned little girl and how long it took to treat her. I recall one of the first Indian deliveries in the hospital, the wife of the young chief. He sat on a chair next to his wife during the delivery (something that not many husbands did in those days) and would lean over occasionally to tell her how she was doing. The next morning, when I went to give her breakfast, she was gone. Looking through the window I saw the two of them walking across the river to their tent with the baby. (Incidentally, theirs was the first Indian wedding I ever attended. She was a beautiful girl and Joseph was tall and handsome. They had lovely handmade moccasins and deerskin jackets. After the ceremony, a fire was built outside and there was a dance around the fire. We joined in with the dancing and the chanting.) Then there was the time my sister came in to have her baby. The nurse told me to go to bed and she would call me if she needed me. I lay there and heard every sound from the room where my sister was in labour. Finally I heard the baby cry. A while after, when the nurse opened my door I pretended to be asleep. I heard her say to the doctor, "These people don't worry about much, do they?" I waited until they went downstairs and then I crept out to see my new niece and stayed with my sister, who knew that I would be awake and would come to her after the doctor and nurse had left.

Each spring we cleaned ceilings, walls, floors and whatever else there was to clean in the hospital. One spring, after we had finished a fairly large staff room, one of the staff turned the mantle lamp a bit too high and the next morning the room was black with soot. With much laughter and hard work we eventually got everything clean again. I remember that room very well, because I spent much of my time there. It was a very pleasant room with comfortable seats, couches and flowers in the window. I took great pride in keeping it nice. When I was finished one day, the housekeeper came to ask me if I had seen some money which she had left on the mantelpiece. When I told her I hadn't, she insisted that I must have since no one else had been there. I knew then that she suspected me of taking it. I felt heartsick and ashamed that anyone would think that I would steal. If my family heard of this they would be very upset. Although I was sixteen, I could not control myself. I cried and sobbed all morning as I went about my work. I waited on tables with red and swollen eyes. Later in the afternoon, the housekeeper came and told me that was enough crying now. She said she had found the money. She had placed it somewhere else. The staff were not always careful how they spoke to us Labrador girls, mostly because they knew nothing of our way of life and the way we were taught at home.

I remember with pleasure the summer I was chosen to go to the Indian Harbour hospital as a ward aide. Each summer the doctor at North West River left the hospital in charge of the nurse and moved to Indian Harbour with some of the staff, to care for the Newfoundland fishermen. Indian Harbour is on a bare rock of an island near the mouth of Hamilton Inlet. The cliff rocks formed a shape like the head and torso of a sleeping Indian, hence its name.

I enjoyed every minute of that summer. As a ward aide I got to see a lot of Dr. Huntington, an American, who took pains to help and encourage me. The nurse was also an American, and was very kind as well. I began to think that this America must be a wonderful place.

Indian Harbour was a good safe harbour for the fishing fleet and was very busy during the summer. There was quite a bit of surgery done there. It seemed that I spent a lot of time cleaning up the operating room (O.R.), soaking bloody linen, cleaning instruments and cleaning furniture and floors for the next set of operations. Every coastal boat that came brought more patients. My younger brother and sister came that summer to have their tonsils removed. When they came out of the O.R. with their faces full of blood and looking so pale, I was frightened. I hid my fear and sat with them until they awakened and then went on to the next patient.

There was a tiny church at Indian Harbour where the "floater" fishermen from the schooners and the few fisherfolk from nearby islands would attend services, conducted by Dr. Paddon or Dr. Huntington; Sunday afternoons there would be prayers on the wards. We would move all the patients into one ward, and all the workers were expected to attend as well. Whenever I had any spare time I would go to the little laundry that sat on a rock not far from the hospital. There I could help Aunt Kitty tin bakeapples.

It was at Indian Harbour that I watched my first patient die. It left me with many questions in my mind. He was a young man of 18 who had come down from Newfoundland with his parents for the fishing season. He became ill suddenly and was taken to the hospital partially unconscious. I watched and held him while the doctor did a spinal puncture to confirm his diagnosis of meningitis. I saw the agony on his mother's face as she watched over him. The doctor could do nothing for him. He died when I was alone with him. I called the doctor when his breathing stopped, wondering why he had to die and if he could have been saved somewhere else. I also wondered if I would catch the meningitis, because I was always by his bed. I could see the doctor was upset so I didn't ask him about it. I worried for a while, but as the days passed and I kept well, I forgot about my fears for myself. I have never forgotten about that poor young man.

When the summer ended we headed back to North West River. Passing through Rigolet I was able to see my family for a few moments. I wished I could stay at home for a longer visit, because I felt that I was missing seeing my brothers and sisters grow up. After all, from the time I was ten I was only able to come home for brief visits. There were some of my eight brothers and sisters that I scarcely saw when they were children. But, then again, I was earning my own way and I knew that meant a lot to my family.

Back in North West River, I went on happily about my work, which by now was routine. One day Dr. Paddon told me that the Mission would find some way to help me train in America if I really wanted to become a nurse. I scarcely dared to hope that they would find someone who would take me. By this time my salary was five dollars a month, a great improvement over fifty cents, but I knew I could not save enough to pay for my education. Because of my upbringing, however, I was ashamed that I might have to take charity from the Mission. Perhaps I could work really hard when I got back as a nurse

44

and help, in some way, to repay the debt.

During my last year at North West River I turned eighteen. Many of my friends were getting married and starting families. I wanted a family very much, but I knew that for me a family would have to wait.

One day, late in spring, Dr. Paddon and Nurse Peterson called me in and told me that Miss Peterson was going home that summer to take a job as a school nurse in Madison, Wisconsin. If I were willing to put up with what she had, I could stay with her and she would feed me. She would also be able to enroll me in a school. If you remember, I had only gone to the ninth grade, and in order to receive training, I would have to complete the twelfth grade.

My joy knew no bounds, and yet I was afraid to talk much about my hopes, so life at the hospital went on as usual. When the nurse left on the first boat, I told myself that was the last I would see of her. But, in midsummer I was told I would be going to St. Anthony to get ready to go to the States, but first I could go home to be with my family for a while. At home all we talked about was my future. I was very proud when people came in and Ma told them I was going away to train to be a nurse. She always added, "She thinks she can be a nurse, but I don't know how she'll get along. I could never make a lady out of her." I could tell that she and Pa were pleased that I was going to make something of myself. Oddly enough, when the day came for me to leave, and we saw the smoke over Lester's Point, I became very upset and burst into tears.

At St. Anthony the IGA put me to work as an aide, to gain experience. Miss Carlson was still there and took great interest in my preparation. Once I had to go to St. John's to have X-rays and obtain a passport. This was the first time I had gone beyond St. Anthony. I was met by a Grenfell worker and taken around St. John's. I was amazed at the size of the town. I saw horses pulling sleighs over cobblestones instead of grass and wondered where all the people could have come from. I slept at the YWCA, where the girls were very friendly, but one night they had a good laugh at my expense. The phone rang and they told me to answer it. When the voice on the other end asked for one of the girls, I said, "Just a moment" very politely. Then I hung up. The girls then told me that hanging up cuts off the caller and we had a good laugh. I told myself I was going to make a lot of boo-boos, so I might as well be prepared to laugh at myself with the others.

Back at St. Anthony I continued to enjoy aide work, content and at home. Late in August Miss Carlson told me I would soon be leaving for St. John's where I would catch a boat to Boston, Massachusetts. There I would be met by an American lady, an IGA teacher who I knew from North West River, who would set me on my way to Madison. The S.S. *Nova Scotia* sailed from St. John's on September 4, 1933. She seemed to me to be a floating palace. You were waited on hand and foot. On deck people were playing some kind of game with sticks. Everywhere there were people sitting around on deck chairs with stewards bringing them hot chocolate or tea. I thought all the other passengers must be very rich to be able to travel this way.

It was daylight when we pulled into Boston Harbour and I just didn't know where to look. There were houses everywhere. Some of the buildings were so high that you had to crane your neck to see the sky. Cars were going in every direction, and I couldn't understand why they weren't crashing into each other. I wondered how I would get to shore safely. All the passengers had to go through a little room before going ashore. While I was in the line, I heard my name being called, but I couldn't see who was calling. I was very afraid. How did these people know my name? What kind of trouble was I in? When I reached the customs and immigration officer I told him I was Miss Blake. He asked why I hadn't come forward before, as there was a lady waiting for me on the dock. Looking down I saw Miss Lorimer, the first familiar face I had seen since I left St. Anthony. I swallowed the lump in my throat and tried to look independent and at home. The car ride to Miss Lorimer's home in Chicopee was sheer amazement. Everything was clean and organized. The grass was cut, there were flowers everywhere and there were fancy trees. We were riding on a smooth hard surface and people were walking along strips of the same material (I had never seen concrete before). There were high poles everywhere with little wires running from one building to another and you always saw them when you looked up. It took most of the day to drive from Boston to Chicopee. I spoke very little because I was so busy looking. Miss Lorimer showed me certain points of interest, but the things she took for granted as being of no particular interest were just as fascinating. For instance, I remember being both fascinated and confused by the way that all the grass on people's lawns had somehow been cut the same height.

When we arrived at Miss Lorimer's home, I was very kindly received by her parents. She took me around the yard to see the flowers and trees. There was a real fruit tree there. She let me pick a fruit to eat. I think it was a pear tree — I had only seen pears in tins and I had no idea that they grew this way. I found the meals strange, but I politely ate them, because I knew I would have to get used to the different foods "outsiders" ate. The meats were good but most of the vegetables were new to me.

The next day, Miss Lorimer told me how I was to proceed to Madison. I would have to change trains at a place called Chicago and go to Madison on another train. I was instructed that I wasn't to speak to everybody I met, as we did at home. There were people who helped passengers; I should go to them. She explained how they would be dressed. I could also ask a policeman for help. I took a good look at a policeman's uniform and at the travellers' aid officer, so I would know who to call on for help. When Miss Lorimer took me to the station, there were black men with red caps coming right toward us. One took my suitcase from the car and carried it into the station and held out his hand. I didn't catch on. Miss Lorimer gave him some money and when he had gone she explained tipping to me. Then she gave me some money in case I should need it.

All during the train ride I sat glued to the window. We went very fast. Sometimes the wheels sounded like they were singing and other times like groaning. At night it was very comfortable. Beds came down from the walls and underneath the seats made more beds, each had a curtain.

Arriving in Chicago was very scary to me. There were even more people of all colours and kinds. I hurried to find a travellers' aid who got someone to take me to the next train and saw me settled aboard. I had been told that someone would call out the names of the places as we arrived, so I listened carefully for Madison. I was getting used to the train, but how I wished I had someone from home to share all these wonders with! All the people around me seemed so disinterested and were reading books and papers rather than looking out the window. Sometimes fields would flash by and sometimes farms with all kinds of birds and animals, and always there were houses and people. I wished there was a way to slow the train sometimes so that I could take a closer look.

The Saturday afternoon that I arrived in Madison was perhaps the hottest day that summer. I was very uncomfortable on the train. As we arrived I saw Miss Peterson from the window. She was the nurse I had worked with in North West River and with whom I was to stay. She surely looked beautiful to me. What a feeling of relief to know that I had finally reached my destination.

Miss Peterson lived in a tiny apartment with one small bed/living room, a tiny bathroom and a cubby-hole kitchen. It was one of these apartments that have shops downstairs and a few offices. There were a couple of school teachers and us upstairs. You knew the names of the people around you because it was written on their door, but you didn't speak to them when you met them in the hall or on the stairs. I found this very strange. After I had been living there about six months I got to know the lady across the hall from us.

I slept on a mattress on the floor, which in the day was placed on top of Miss Peterson's bed, then used as a couch. When the mattress was on the floor there was very little room to move around. I slept scarcely at all that first night. My head was buzzing with all the things that I was supposed to remember. I was a bit worried about going to school the next morning. Here I was, eighteen years old and just beginning high school with children who were thirteen and fourteen. I was sure they would all think I was pretty stupid. Next morning I left for school early. I stood on the street across from the school until some children came along, then I crossed the street when they did. Finding the principal's office, I was given a locker number and a key, and the number of my homeroom. Our homeroom teacher gave us seats, told us where to get our books and informed us we would spend the day getting things ready. We made a chart for the week's schedule. A different room and a different teacher for each subject! You always came to your homeroom first thing in the morning and when you had a free period for study.

After everything was organized my teacher, Miss Wilson, said, "I am handing out a short test paper. It is to see how well you know your country." I nearly wept when I saw the questions. I didn't even know what the President's name was, what a silo was or where the Windy City was. In fact, I could only answer one. (I did know who the King of England was). I worried while Miss Wilson was going over the papers. I was sure I didn't know enough to get into the ninth grade. When the teacher dismissed the class, she asked me to stay behind. She was kind and understanding when she found out where I was from and she told me not to worry. She gave me another test, mostly about the three R's, and found that I was quite able to get into the ninth grade. The next morning she told the rest of the class where I had come from and they were all most interested. They asked many questions about Labrador and our way of life there. Miss Wilson must have told the other teachers about the new girl from Labrador, because they were all most kind and patient and very, very helpful.

That week I got to know a few of the students in my classes and they seemed to accept me as one of them. For a long time I was busy every minute, trying to cope with my new life, studying hard at night to catch up with the rest of the class. The American children seemed so sophisticated and I felt so naive, although I was four years older. The students seemed to feel equal to the teachers and talked freely with them. They spoke up in class without shyness. I very quickly gave up saying, "Yes, Miss" and "No, Miss" when I saw the looks I got from the other students. All the girls dressed well, wore makeup and had their hair done. Sometimes I felt very out of place.

Gradually I began to meet other people; mothers and fathers of some of my new friends and friends of Miss Peterson. I went to see movies a few times, learned how to use buses, got to know my way downtown to look in the store windows and began to like some of the new foods. I thought America must be a beautiful country, if every place was like Madison. The houses and yards were so big and well cared for. There were houses everywhere and you had to walk a long way to find a lake or some woods.

I became used to the everyday things that had seemed so strange to me at first; coloured people everywhere, people riding bicycles and meeting crowds of people every day. When I went to the movies I heard the expression "Nigger Heaven" (which described the cheap seats in the balcony). I immediately disliked the expression. In fact I was generally disappointed that otherwise sensible people looked down on the blacks. Although I had never seen Negroes before it was no secret to me that many people had skin a different colour from mine. We were perhaps not very advanced in Labrador, but I had always been taught at home that all people are equal. There were a few black children in our school and I liked them very much, but I did notice that they kept to their own group a lot.

It was late December by the time I got used to this new life and caught up with my classmates and, finally, had some spare time. Suddenly I got desperately homesick. I had only heard from home once, due to the isolation of Labrador and the route the mail had to come. Elliot Merrick, a teacher who had been in North West River while I was there, wrote a book about his trip to the trapping grounds and had sent me a copy for Christmas. The names in the book were all familiar and some were relatives. I read my one letter and that book over and over, night after night, after Miss Peterson had gone to sleep. Physically, I was a grown woman, but I had never known such despair and loneliness. I felt that if only I could get home I would never leave Labrador again. During the day I forced myself to study and keep busy, but oh, the nights were lonely. That first winter was really tough.

Miss Peterson must have noticed my sadness, because one day in the spring she told me she had written to the Hudson's Bay company to inquire about my getting passage on their boat *Naskaupi*, which sailed down the St. Lawrence River and on to all the HBC posts in Labrador. This chance to see home kept me going all spring. About the time I was studying for final exams, I received a letter from the HBC, saying that they would give me passage from Montreal to Rigolet and back to Montreal in the fall. My joy knew no bounds. I buckled down, determined to do well in my exams. By this time I had found a way to make a little pocket money. I had been asked to tell a church group about Labrador. Then, other groups began to ask me to speak to them, sometimes offering some small payment. I spoke to school and church groups and very carefully looked after my money. I was able to save a little and, now that I was going home, I could bring some little things to my family. By the time I was ready to leave I knew I had passed the exams and could go on to grade ten. I told myself, "Once you get home you will never come back".

When I boarded the *Naskaupi* in Halifax, the first person I saw was a Grenfell Mission worker, Mrs. Keddie, who had been on holiday and was returning to Labrador. I had worked with her at North West River. It was so good to see someone who had been at North West River and knew the people there. The HBC governor and his wife were on the boat as well; they were making a visit to all the HBC posts. They were nice people and we were asked to have tea in their cabin once.

At last we came to Rigolet where I was dropped off to be picked up when the boat returned from her northern trip. What a joy to be home! I rushed around to see everyone that first day and couldn't get enough salmon to eat. Ma cooked seal for me, the way that only she could. Some days I ate seal for dinner, supper and breakfast. Later we went to Mulliauk, where we had a log cabin for salmon fishing. Still later I went to my beloved North West River to visit my married sister and to see all my friends. Once I met Dr. Paddon and he told me he had a report from the school. He said I had done very well that first year and he thought I should work hard, continue going to school to prove I could succeed and justify the faith of those who had helped me. After all, it was very unusual for a Labrador girl to be getting the kind of education that I was. I know of only one Labrador girl before me who had received nurse's training, although I think there were one or two others continuing their education in the United States at the same time I was in Madison.

By the time the *Naskaupi* was due back, I had made up my mind that I would go back to the United States. I did not want to disappoint my family or those who believed in me, but most of all I did not want to let go of my ambition to become a nurse.

8a. Snowshoeing on a day off.

8b. Hospital staff leaving NW River for Indian Harbour. Dr Harry Paddon is in the foreground.

CHAPTER FOUR

Nurse's Training

I returned to Madison a couple of weeks late for the beginning of school. I decided I could get through high school in three and a half years instead of four and my teachers agreed. I knew that then there would be three years of training before I became a nurse. I was now determined that I would stick to my ambition and I could not visit home again until I was finished, so I faced six more years before I could go home again! I couldn't bear thinking about it.

Fortunately, in my second year of school, I was invited by the mother of my friend, Judy, to live with them. This was the best thing that could have happened for me at that time. I was a member of a family again, and what a family the Feltons were! I soon called Mr. and Mrs. Felton "Pop" and "Mom". The Feltons were of German descent and Pop was a truck-garden farmer. I learned much from these people about the American way of life. Had I remained in the United States I think I would have been most content to live on a farm. What a pleasure it was to go out and gather fresh eggs, watch the cows being milked and help yourself to the vegetables. There was a grape arbour there and when Judy and I were studying we would reach up once in a while to pick a bunch of grapes. It seemed like the garden of Eden to me. I remained with that family for the rest of my high-school years.

I finished high school in three and a half years, as I had planned. The last year I was inducted into the National Honors Society. I still proudly wear my pin today. On graduation day I thought a lot about my family in Labrador and how proud they would have been to see me in my cap and gown. All my classmates brought their parents and other relatives. Mom and Pop Felton came with me.

By this time I was enjoying America and this new way of life. But always in the back of my mind was the thought that I would be returning to Labrador as a nurse. During high school I had been hearing from home about once every four or five months. I never knew how the family was until I received one of the much-worn letters. I kept on talking to groups about Labrador. I really didn't like these speaking engagements and would be happy when I could earn money in other ways. Many people knew so little about Labrador that I was sure they felt that I was making most of it up.

With my high school diploma in my hands the next thing to do was apply to a school of nursing and earn enough money for entry into the school. A good friend I had met through church had a sister in Duluth, Minnesota, who thought I would like it there because of the cold climate. (It was obvious to my friends that I was very uncomfortable in Madison during warm weather.) I got some names of Minnesota training schools, selected and applied to St. Luke's Hospital School for Nurses in Duluth. In my letter I asked if there was some job I could do to earn the twenty-five dollar entry fee. As the summer slipped my worry mounted each day that I did not hear from St. Luke's. Finally, late in the summer, I received a letter saying that the September class was filled, but if I didn't mind waiting I could be accepted for the January class. In addition, I could have a job as maid there while I was waiting for classes to begin. The letter stated that I could start the job right away.

Everything that I owned went back into the same small cardboard suitcase I had when I left home, now getting somewhat frayed. When I arrived at Duluth, my friend's sister met me and took me to her home. She had offered to get me settled in Duluth. Once again I was unbelievably lucky. Another family took me as one of their own and my friend's sister and her husband became my beloved Aunt Ida and Uncle Walter. For the next three years their home was open to me whenever I needed the comforts of a family.

Aunt Ida helped me find the hospital, where I talked with the Personnel Director. She told me my job would be mopping floors on one of the seven floors of the hospital and to do whatever my supervisor asked of me. The salary was such that I would be able to pay my rent, buy a few needed articles of clothing and still save enough for the entrance fee.

Almost immediately I met several other girls who were already working at the hospital. One had found an apartment but couldn't swing the rent, so she asked two of us to go in with her. The room was just across from the hospital and would save us bus fare. We moved in on Sunday. There were three cots in the one room and one chair; no clothes closet, just hooks on the wall. There was a tiny nook where there was an electric cooking ring and a small cupboard. To us it was a shelter, a place to start from until we could afford something better. Our living arrangements were nothing fancy, but I was comfortable in the knowledge that my training would start in a few months.

Two of us started work on the same floor, each being responsible for one-half of the floor, which was divided by the nursing station and the waiting room. There were about twenty rooms for each of us. We were responsible for cleaning out all the toilets, washing the window sills and radiators, chairs and dressers, and wet mopping all the floors. The first day I worried about how I could do all that had to be done and how I would be able to manage the heavy mop all day. It was really tough going. Our days were long and there were no coffee breaks. It took every minute of the day to get all the work done. We had a half-hour lunch break at noon. However, as is the case with all routines, I soon learned the quickest and most efficient way to do things.

Every evening we arrived back at the apartment, flopped on our beds and rested. Gradually we gathered things about us to improve the appearance of our quarters. The first thing I did was save up the twenty-five dollars I needed for the entry fee. Then I helped the others buy things for the apartment.

After I got used to the heavy bucket and mop, I really enjoyed my work. I had forgotten the atmosphere of a hospital — it was almost like going home, and I really enjoyed working with the patients. Of course, you didn't talk to the patients, only to wish them good morning or to answer them if they spoke to you. We weren't allowed to do anything for the patients, other than fetch a nurse. Still, I learned a lot just listening to the patients and the nurses talking while I went about cleaning the toilets. If a maid was in a room when a doctor or nurse came she was supposed to leave, but sometimes when I heard the doctors coming on their rounds I would go into the toilet and pretend to be cleaning so I could listen to them talking. I didn't understand all the medical terms, but I learned some things about medicine and about bedside manner. I thought then, and I still think the same, that the doctors' visits were too often an embarrassment to the patients. The professionals stand around the bed and discuss the patients' ailments and treatments using words the patients don't understand and which sometimes frighten and worry them. I especially wondered about this sort of talk by the bedside of an unconscious patient, for who knows how aware unconscious people are of their surroundings?

I closely watched the student nurses that I saw every day, hoping to get some idea what would be in store for me in a few months. The newest students were the probationers (called "Probies" by the nurses). You would hear a nurse say "Send me a Probie to clean the utility room", or "Straighten the linen room", or "Wash that bedpan". Some of the Probies' tasks did not seem that glamorous, but I was sure I could handle it. After all, I was already cleaning out toilets.

The students wore pretty blue uniforms with white collars, cuffs and stockings. They had little white caps on their heads and were always spotlessly clean. Our uniforms were an ugly green and were always wet and grimy at the end of the day. When my six months as a maid drew to an end I bought white shoes, stockings, shoe polish, toothpaste, a white sweater and a couple of small gifts for the two girls I had lived with for the past five months, and from whom I learned a lot about the American working girl's life.

The day I had waited for so long arrived in the middle of January, 1937. With approximately thirty other girls, I entered Emily Payne Hall, the residence for St. Luke's School for Nurses. It was a magic day for me. We were all measured for our uniforms, given bed linen, instructions and taken to our quarters. In that first week, we were given all kinds of inoculations, complete physicals, got our uniforms fitted, got our text books and were taken on a tour of the hospital. We learned the Rules and Regulations Book by heart. We rose at 6:00 a.m. and had breakfast finished by 6:45 a.m. Then all the nurses gathered in the sitting room of the residence for morning prayers and inspection. Following the singing of a hymn and prayers, the Director of Nursing and her assistant stood at each side of the door. As we all passed through anyone who had dirty shoes, hair touching her collar, wrinkled clothes or bright nail polish was sent to her room to make amends before appearing on duty.

Our work day began at 7:00 a.m. and ended at 7:00 p.m., or when you got your allotted assignments completed. We received five dollars a month throughout the three years of training; this was to help us with pocket money.

The first four months was the probationary period, and we were the lowest of the low. Much of the day was spent in the classroom and many evenings were spent in the library. At first we seldom went out at night, but gradually the need for outside activities became apparent. We walked nearly everywhere because we didn't often have bus fare. Occasionally we went to a movie, then, because we had to be in by five minutes to ten, we ran all the way home from downtown to the hospital. We arrived out of breath, but always under the wire. Lights out was at ten o'clock, so often I washed and brushed my teeth in the dark. You never knew when the housemother was making her rounds and you didn't want her to see a light under your door. On occasions there would be an inspection of your room. Perhaps you would return to your room to find a note on your bed complimenting you on your tidiness or chastising you because of the disorder. We were all very careful during our probationary period. We knew that at the end of that time there would be examinations, reports would be given by the supervisors of the floors on which you had worked, and there would be character references from the housemothers. We were told from the first that all classes were carefully weeded out. At the end of four months only those who were expected to be good nurses were kept on. On the floors everybody knew you were a probationer, so you got all the jobs no one else wanted. You cleaned all the bedpans, fixed flowers, cleaned lockers, answered bells and, all the while, I looked longingly at the nurses, who spent their time with the patients rather than with bedpans. In the classroom we bathed each other, gave needles to, bandaged, massaged and hot packed each other. We learned how to make up dosages of drugs, how to handle and talk to patients and to other staff. We spent hours at our microscopes and dissection tables. After the years that it had taken me to get this far I was finally learning the things that a Labrador nurse would need to know.

We studied hard for our exams and yearned to be accepted into the final class. On the day when the names of those chosen were posted I was thrilled to see my name. However, that was a day of mixed feelings, for some of my friends were leaving, brokenhearted and crying. I wept along with them.

A capping ceremony was held for each class that had completed its probationary period and all the girls' parents came. Aunt Ida and Uncle Walter stood in for my parents. It was an evening to remember. Our caps were placed on our heads by the Director of Nursing, who was respected and loved by us all. Now we were able to do real nursing work!

By now we had established a pattern that we would follow for the next three years. In those days nurses worked twelve-hour shifts and had one day off a week. Some of the girls thought they would never be able to stick it for that long and, indeed, some didn't. I never had the slightest doubt that I would be able to make it through the full three years. Only occasionally I would doubt myself, usually during bouts of homesickness, when the others would be gone home for holidays.

By the end of the first year most of us had boyfriends, although social life was not high on the scale of important things. We chose our boyfriends carefully. It was preferable that he had a job, a car and could dance. We had one late leave a week which meant we could stay out until five to midnight. If you could maneuver your boyfriend to take you to dinner, to an early movie and then to a dance, you were the envy of all. I was able to buy very little clothes. The other girls' parents would send them clothes occasionally and they would stock up each year when they went home on holidays. My classmates were good to me and let me borrow their clothes. Once, after I had saved up for a long time, I bought a beautiful red wool dress and a pair of red shoes. That dress — what it did for us all! I'm sure it was worn at one time or another by everyone in the class.

Every day I learned something new, although many of the treatments we used then are never seen today. I remember once seeing leeches used on a patient. Nurses were also taught to "cup" people with chest infections. You spread Vaseline over the patient's chest, back and front, then placed a small piece of cotton wool into the bottom of the medicine glass. The wool was lit to create a vacuum in the glass and then you quickly placed it mouth down on the patient's flesh and left it until the fire died out. When you removed the glass, little red circles would show where the glass had been, but you never burned the patient. You also used "stupes" a lot. A stupe was a cloth square with sticks through the hem on each end on which you placed boiling hot flannels, used to make hot packs. It took two people to wring the flannels by twisting the sticks.

You worked hard during the twelve-hour shifts, only sitting down while recording information on a patient's chart. Each day your assignments were posted, probably five or six patients to each nurse. You were responsible for the total care of your patients all day, from the time before breakfast, when you washed them and prepared them for eating, until after they had supper and were settled away for the night. I enjoyed the times when I had the same patients for a week or more. Then you were able to develop good nursing care plans and a good relationship with the patients.

Students would do a "rotation" in a different area of medicine (or "specialty") each month. All the specialties were in the same hospital except psychiatry. It was always exciting to start nursing in a new area, to put what was studied in class into practice on the floors, under the watchful eye of the supervisor. One of the few specialties that I didn't like was dietetics, which involved planning and preparing patients' meals. Perhaps this was a carry over from my early dislike of cooking. When you were on diets, you had to do the complete procedure. If you were studying a disease that required special meals, like diabetes, then you planned the patients' diet for the three meals, were checked by your supervisor, weighed all the foods, cooked them and served them to the diabetic patients. Those poor patients. I'm sure their food wasn't always very tasty, at least not when I was preparing it! There was a side benefit to working in the diet kitchen: you could sneak an apple, a few biscuits or a piece of cheese in your apron pocket and have it for a snack later on.

Night shift was not much different from day work. You just ran all night, rather than during the daylight. At times, when the patients were asleep, you had to clean the utility rooms, the linen rooms and the drug cupboards. If you could get a good routine going, and get well organized, you probably got off on time. However, when you were first assigned to a new ward you could count on being an hour or two late getting off in the morning. After one month of supervised night duty you went on alone. The first time I went on alone I was in the tuberculosis wing. It was so spooky in that wing, which was an old part of the hospital. TB patients slept a lot, so it was quiet, but there was a stairway from the TB floor to the roof and on windy nights there was a rattling in that stairway. Chills went down my spine every time I passed that darkened area. While the patients slept, I cleaned the sputum cups, sterilized bedpans, folded linen and did all the other routine things. On that ward I actually looked forward to the supervisor's visit, to have someone to talk to.

I was sure that I had found my niche when I first nursed on pediatrics. How I enjoyed the children, especially the beautiful little black children. Children forgive so easily if they have been hurt with a treatment or an injection and many important pediatric treatments were quite enjoyable for the nurse. Children don't fear or worry about illness or death like adults sometimes do. They could be picked up and cuddled, which works better than a lot of medicines. Reading to them, playing with them or singing to them are all great treatments. No matter how low you feel or how heartbroken you feel about a particular child, who may have a serious injury or incurable illness, you treat them all the same, with love and laughter. The youngest patient will sense that something is not right when they are singled out for special treatment. I was very happy working with children, but, at times, devastated by their suffering.

On obstetrics I found another niche, especially my month in the newborn nursery. There were no midwives in the hospital I trained in, so all nurses were taught how to deliver babies. I paid careful attention, for I knew that this was a skill which was much needed in Labrador. There was always an obstetrician in attendance, so you had a chance to learn the most modern methods. In the classroom we practiced on "Mrs. Chase", a lifelike training model. Very quickly I learned how to examine mothers and determine the progress of labour. One of the things that I liked about obstetrics was that once assigned to an obstetrical patient you stayed with the mother, giving her comfort and encouragement until the birth was over and post-delivery was complete. It was a joyful place to work.

I had not been a student very long before word got around to the doctors that I would be going back to Labrador to nurse, where doctors were scarce and nurses were often alone. They went out of their way to help me. One doctor let me help him with all of his deliveries, so that I would have some experience with all kinds of difficult births under his supervision.

When I was assigned to the newborn nursery I knew I would never want to leave. Each nurse was assigned to five or six babies. What a pleasure to care for them! A lot of their care was cuddling. At that time all mothers breast-fed their babies. The babies were fed every four hours, except for small or premature babies who were fed every three hours, or as the doctor ordered. You would start your shift with the newborns by making a trip to the mothers with the breast tray to prepare them for the babies and see that they were comfortable. Each baby was then weighed and brought to the mother, so you could help the mother start feeding before moving on to the next. By the time all six babies were weighed, brought and set feeding, it was time to visit the first mother, get the baby, bring it back to the nursery, weigh it and change it. The nursery was an extremely busy place: washing babies and mothers, changing gowns, changing babies and keeping records was a cycle that never seemed to end. However, there were always times during the twelve-hour shift when you would pick up the babies to cuddle them, sing to them and rock them. My time on that rotation flew much too quickly.

By the end of my second year's training many of the rotations were complete. My classmates and I were much more confident and were quite capable of running a floor alone or with a student. At first I found it a great burden to be in charge of anybody, even a "Probie", but, with the help of the supervisor, I soon gained confidence and became quite efficient at organizing and carrying out duties.

Once, near the end of the night-duty tour, I had a really devastating experience. The aunt of one of our classmates was admitted for abdominal surgery. She recovered normally and we became friends. Her family would come during visiting hours and all would have a happy time. She was so grateful for the little things the nurses had done for her, that she made plans to have us visit her at her home. The evening I took the report and learned that she was to go home the next day, I felt happy for her. Rounds to all patients were made every hour. At six in the morning she was awake and asked for the bedpan. Returning a few minutes later, I found her gasping and turning blue. The supervisor and the doctor came immediately at my call. No amount of resuscitation or treatment could help. She died of an embolism, or blocked blood vessel.

We had been told that when a patient died we were to carry on as usual and continue our work with a cheerful smile, for the sake of the family and the other patients. I believed that most people who have lost a relative are more comforted by genuine sympathy than by phrases like "It's all for the best" or "She's not suffering now". The patients are people and can appreciate that nurses are people as well. They could understand if they saw a nurse weeping a little or looking sad.

There was only one rotation that I never did get used to, and that was psychiatry. We took our training in nursing patients with mental diseases and disorders at a state institution in St. Peter, Minnesota, nearly a day's drive from St. Luke's. All the buildings of the institution were surrounded by a high fence. Once we were inside that fence every door entered had to be unlocked and then locked again, and you had better not forget to do it. I sometimes felt like a prisoner there, so I can only imagine how the patients felt. Some of the patients were criminally insane and had done quite serious crimes, like rapes or murders. Others were less disturbed, but often their faces were so blank and so hopeless. There were also patients who were only mildly ill and some of them would not be in mental hospitals today.

When I arrived back at St. Luke's I was called to the nursing director's office. She told me that I had passed psychiatry, but that she was wondering why my grades were so much lower than usual. I had to tell her that I felt we had not been helping the patients very much. I did not like any kind of nursing where I felt that my efforts were not helping patients get well, or at least become more comfortable with their illness.

By the time I reached the third year of training the end was in sight. As seniors my classmates and I were now depended upon to do much of the nursing care in the hospital. We also took care of the floor to relieve the head nurse, and we were capable of running things and directing the juniors in a responsible manner. We took much pride in our work. This was a time when there were changes taking place in nursing in the United States. There had been talk for a long time of nurses doing eight-hour shifts. During the last few months of our training this came about. This gave us a lot more time off and at first we scarcely knew what to do with all the time. The realization soon came that in a few months we would be writing our State Board examinations, so we found a way to fill the hours.

My last rotation was contagion. All the patients with diseases that were very catching were on the one wing, an interesting and challenging place to work. Again, I liked the children best of all. One particular child stole my heart, a little black girl with whom I spent every spare minute. She didn't like the mask I had to wear and whenever I went near her she pulled it off. She was clearly a much-loved child at home and needed to be cuddled a lot, since she was only occasionally allowed to be with her parents. So, of course, I developed a very severe case of measles and lost three weeks of duty time. All sick leave had to be made up before you could "go into white" as a qualified nurse at the end of the training period. Our three years were up the middle of January and on that day only one or two nurses went in white, while the rest of us had to wait out our sick days.

As a graduate I was able to take a job at the hospital in the area of my choice, if there was an opening. To my delight I was posted back to pediatrics. Knowing that we would write our final State exams to become Registered Nurses in the spring, I wrote to the Grenfell Mission office in New York, stating that I hoped to be a registered nurse soon and I wished to go back with the IGA in Labrador. When the application forms arrived, of course, I applied to go to the North West River hospital. I looked forward to returning home to see my family and to fulfill my destiny as a nurse in Labrador.

9b. On the Kyle on my way home. l-r: John Paddon, nurse Mona Kelland, myself and Mina Paddon.

9a. A group of student nurses at the State Hospital for the Insane in Minnesota.

10a. A photo that Ma sent me while I was away at school. She put the initials of my brothers and sisters above their heads, so I could recognize them!

10b. Sterilizing instruments for the O.R. at St. Anthony.

CHAPTER FIVE

Back Home

While I was waiting to write the State Board examinations, I made my plans to go home. I had one setback, just before the beginning of exams, when I got a letter from the IGA office in New York. The Mission was pleased to hire me, but could not send me to North West River. Replacement workers were badly needed in Labrador, for this was 1940 and many medical people were leaving the mission to join the services, so I could hardly abandon my duty, just because I was not going to get the hospital that I wanted. I was crestfallen, but decided to accept their offer to go to Cartwright; at least I would be in Labrador and would have a better chance of getting to North West River at some time in the near future. I still have the contract that I signed, for a salary of $350 per year, less ten per cent. The letter from the IGA also informed me that I would have to leave early in order to connect with the coastal boat on July 1. So the mission set a date for me to leave Duluth, June 20th. Our graduation ceremony was to be held on June 30th. Of course I agreed to go, but I have always regretted missing that ceremony.

Examinations came in the spring and consisted of two parts: an oral exam before the Board of Directors of the hospital and a written exam set by the State Board Examiner of Nurses. On the day of the oral exam, we all met and sat outside the Board Room. We were called in alphabetically; as my name was Blake I went in early. I sat there shaking in my shoes. My mind seemed to go blank. At last my name was called. There was a long table in the Board Room and at one end sat the chairman, flanked on each side by members of the Board. Also present were the Director of Nursing, her assistant and our teacher. All alone at the other end was a chair for the student. I answered the questions asked but came away feeling I had done very badly, for as soon as I was out of the room I thought of much more that I could have said.

With the orals behind us, we started to study in earnest for the State boards. How much we had crammed into the last three years! How were we to remember it all? The evenings during the last month before exams were spent studying. We would study a subject and then meet in a group and answer questions. How was it possible to remember all those incubation periods, the names of all the nerves, the different kinds of cells and what drugs were used to treat what diseases? There would be endless questions during those several days of written examinations. It was a time of anxiety and sometimes despair as I thought of what it would mean to me if I failed. I couldn't go home until I became a registered nurse, no matter how long it took.

One day, just before the State Boards, the results of the orals were posted; to those of us who had passed it was great encouragement. The written exams themselves were a trial I would just as soon forget. Each night we crammed for the subject coming up the next day, and each subject we wrote on I was sure I had failed.

After the written exams we threw ourselves back into our work. Sometimes we would forget about the examinations, for it usually took a month or more before the results would be ready. One day as I was sleeping (for I was on night duty) I was awakened by one of my classmates shouting outside my room. "Wake up. Wake up. The results are here. I passed and I have your results here."

I told her to open it and if I failed just slip the envelope under my door and go away.

She shouted, "Milly, you passed. You passed!"

I was up like a bolt and we were dancing, laughing and shouting together. What joy! I would be going home for sure!

Of course, Cartwright was not necessarily home, and I knew it would be quite some time before I was free to visit, but at least I would be near my family. It was seven years since I had seen any of them. But, on that great day, all the sacrifices I had made to become a nurse seemed worthwhile.

For the next few weeks all I could think about was going home. I was now getting paid as a registered nurse and could stock up on things like uniforms, duty stockings and shoes, a few warm clothes for travel, and little things to bring home to my family. At work the days sped by and the evenings were spent saying good-bye to the friends I had made in Duluth.

One evening my classmates took me out to dinner. We had dinner at the Duluth Hotel and there was a popular band playing and, knowing that "In the Mood" was my favourite dance tune, the girls arranged to have it played for me. They also gave me a gardenia to wear, since it was my favourite corsage. Afterward we walked home laughing and talking, and when we arrived back at the Nurses' Residence someone suggested we go to the sitting room and talk for a while. When the doors opened there were shouts of "Surprise! Surprise!". Nurses, doctors and auxiliary staff were there. I stood, while gifts were presented to me, with a large lump in my throat, swallowing back tears. There was a set of luggage, a beautiful nurse's watch and many other useful things. The doctors gave me a doctor's bag, complete with instruments and pill containers. The greatest gift of all was the love and caring that prompted those acts. It sort of made up for missing my graduation. I still have the card with the names of those present.

On the day I left my classmates, who were off duty, accompanied me to the train. I boarded the train with my arms full: a bouquet of flowers and a box of candy and a lunch and gifts packed by Aunt Ida and Uncle Walter.

In Boston I found that I had some hours to wait before I could meet the travelling companions I was expecting, Mrs. Mina Paddon and her son John. Dr. Harry Paddon, whom I had worked with in North West River, had been on winter furlough in the United States and had died suddenly Christmas-time. Mrs. Paddon, who was also a nurse, shared her husband's commitment to Labrador, and was returning to North West River to take charge of the hospital there. When I saw Mrs. Paddon and John walk into the station it was the first time I had seen a familiar face from home in seven years. I remembered John as a baby, then as a two-year-old, and here he was now, a ten-year-old. I wondered if I would know some members of my family when I saw them. Some of them would be men and women. I worried a little about this.

Years before I had heard jokes about Newfoundlanders who had left home to live elsewhere for a few years. I knew that I had changed my speech, trying to fit in the United States. I felt that I hadn't put on any airs (for, after all, a student nurse is not allowed to consider herself too good for very much), but I hoped that I would at least be able to recognize my own people.

Once a girl from Labrador came home from outside to visit her uncle, so the story goes, and she was asking him numerous questions about things that she should have been familiar with. On seeing the caplin roll in, she asked her uncle what all those little fishes were.

"Caplin, you bloody fool," said her uncle, "Like you were reared up on."

So I hoped I hadn't changed too much.

Luckily, the journey back home gradually got me used to the things I could expect at home. We travelled from Boston to Sydney on the train and then went across to Port aux Basques by boat. In Newfoundland the scenery began to get more familiar and homelike: the fishermen out jigging as we approached Port aux Basques, the rocky land and the spruce trees glimpsed from the train. As we travelled to St. John's, I was thrilled every time we passed people carrying water buckets, clothes drying on the lines or people out tending their small gardens. Outside the settlements there were the high hills and green valleys of the beautiful interior, and space, beautiful space, with not a house in sight.

At St. John's we boarded the S.S. *Kyle* for the last leg of the journey home. The captain, stewards and crew greeted and welcomed me like a long-lost friend. Many of them had been on the *Kyle* in the years that I travelled back and forth to attend school. By this time I was no longer worried, but was full of anticipation as we set out for Labrador.

In St. Anthony we docked at two in the morning. Still, I got up to see if there was anyone around that I knew. But only strangers came from the hospital to pick up the patients we had brought in and the rest of the town was asleep. The only familiar face I saw was the man who caught the ropes to secure the boat. We talked and I gave him messages for mutual friends.

When I awoke the next morning the *Kyle* was across the Strait of Belle Isle and moving along the rocky coastline of Labrador. Many times I have read about "the bleak and barren Labrador". Such a description could only be written by a person who never saw the interior. While the coastline that I saw that morning was rocky, there was much beauty to be seen as well. I clung to the rail of the *Kyle*, drinking in the majestic sea-washed cliffs towering over the deep blue sea. I hadn't realized how much I had missed the ocean during my years in Wisconsin and Minnesota. There were small green patches nestled amidst the cliffs, where the fragile summer homes of the fishermen were built. As we travelled up the coast I didn't turn up my nose. I saw beauty and courage and the love of life and home, and I knew I was going back to a people who respect and survive the harshness of the land.

The coastal boat stopped at all the little fishing places along the way. Small boats were soon alongside, bobbing up and down while mail, freight and passengers transferred from one boat to the other. Sometimes the steamer would wait until someone was seen by the nurse, who travelled on the *Kyle* to care for people in isolated places. Sometimes a tooth had to be extracted, or we waited for the patient to go ashore and collect her belongings because she had to be taken to the nearest hospital. Passengers and crew lined the rails and looked down on the little boats, telling people the news from along the coast and what was happening with the war. Then the whistle blew, the little boats departed and it was off to the next harbour for a repeat performance.

Away from the land there was plenty to see as well. You could see whales blowing, seals poking their heads out of the water or dolphins showing off as they wiggled up in the sunshine, sometimes completely out of the water. Sometimes the dolphins would race the boat and the passengers would go to the bow and click their cameras. There were always birds; gulls that followed the boat the whole trip for the tidbits that were thrown overboard. There were ducks, turrs and wild birds of many other species.

As we sailed into Hawke's Harbour the off-shore wind wafted the most horrible smell to the boat. Some time while I was away a whaling station had been built there. We could see whales lying on the slipway. Passengers and tourists went ashore for a closer look. Men walked over the whale while they hacked out huge slabs of blubber, which was hauled by pulley to the storehouse above. The odor was awful. There were stacks of casks filled with oil for shipping, ready to be loaded on a boat anchored in the bay. Rocks, walkways and wharfs were all slippery with fat. When the whistle blew we all went aboard carrying whale meat steaks for supper that night. They were delicious and I knew at once that my love of the traditional foods of Labrador had not left me during my years "outside".

As soon as the boat turned into Sandwich Bay it was as if we had entered another country. Instead of bare rocks, the beautiful high hills were covered with regiments of trees that came right down to the long clean beaches. Here and there I could see a little white summer shack with smoke coming out of the stovepipe and children and dogs playing alongside. This sight, more than any of the others, made me realize that I was home. We turned the point and entered the lovely settlement of Cartwright, spread out on each side of the harbour. On one side was the Hudson's Bay Company store and shed, with houses spread out on each side of the HBC premises. Across the harbour were the imposing buildings of the International Grenfell Association. This was my destination. As we came slowly into the harbour, boats were coming out from the shore in all directions. By the time we anchored we were surrounded. I watched the Mission boat as she came out filled with people, then stood by the railing and watched as the passengers came aboard. One young man looked very familiar. We stared at each other as he came up the ladder. "You wouldn't be Millicent, would you?" he asked. I replied, "Yes. Are you Bruce?", for this fine-looking man was my brother, who I remembered as an imp of a boy. Bruce had been up for tooth extractions and was on his way back home on the *Kyle*. He told me that the family was well, but that my sister Margaret was up in the hospital. We had very little time to talk, for Dr. Forsythe had come to greet me and take me ashore.

On the walk up to the hospital Dr. Forsythe began to tell me about some of the work, the patients and the place. Arriving, he introduced me to the nurse I was to replace, who would be leaving when the boat returned from north. Together we visited the patients. And there in one of the beds was my beloved sister, Margaret. She was as beautiful and as cheerful as I remembered her to be. Oh, it was so good to see family again and to be home among my own people.

My first few days at Cartwright were very busy. Dr. Forsythe was getting ready for his medical trip along the coast in the hospital ship and would be gone for some time. When the doctor and the nurse both left I would be alone, so I crammed as much knowledge into my head as I could, and I began to realize how very little I knew, despite my recently completed training. The hospital's medical books and my textbooks became my only reading. I would be alone and responsible for the administration of the little hospital, the health of the staff and the community. It was a monumental task for a new and inexperienced graduate. I felt my confidence falter as I waved goodbye to the doctor and the nurse a few days later.

I was left alone with one Wop (which was what we called a volunteer worker, WOP stood for Without Pay), and the friendship and encouragement of Mrs. Keddie, who looked after the handicraft department of the IGA. I had known her for years at North West River.

My days were full and I often worked through the night as well. The little hospital was full of patients. The hospital was available to people at all times. In those days there were no set clinic hours, people came when they needed to and were never turned away. As one bed got empty it was filled right away. House calls in the community or the surrounding communities were also attended to whenever the need arose. Occasionally I would get a break and went for a boat ride, a long hike or to visit my aunt and other friends who lived across the harbour. I wanted to visit Muddy Bay, where my school had been, but there was never time.

In the hospital I had one aide, who had been trained on the job, to help care for the patients. Together we did the feeding, bathing and cleaning and the daily running of the wards. I tried to train the aide as we worked, continuing the practice of senior students teaching the juniors that I had learned at nursing school. She was the one who would help while I delivered a baby, help to hold a child while its burns or wounds were dressed or give the needed drugs if I was called away. She became my valued helper and supporter as well as my friend.

The patients and ills were varied. Sometimes fishermen would come in with infected water pups. This was a condition caused by the rubbing of oilskins on the wrists of the fishermen. The result was blisters which broke and became infected. Perhaps someone might have a jigger caught in his hand and it would have to be cut out. There were people who were being treated for tuberculosis. There were patients who were sent in from St. Anthony where they had surgery or casts and they would stay with us until they could be discharged. Each time the boat came there were new patients.

One night, as I met the patients coming from the southbound boat, I was amazed to see my father being brought in on a stretcher. His leg was grossly swollen and on examination I found it to be hot and hard. His fever indicated a full-blown infection. I was very anxious for he was extremely ill. I nursed him day and night and soon saw him begin to improve. He was in the ward with the captain of a Newfoundland fishing schooner. They soon became great friends. One day as I was leaving the ward, I heard my father say, "That's my daughter, you know." The pride that rang in his voice made all the sacrifices worthwhile. After Pa had been in the hospital a week, my mother arrived to see him. What a reunion! I shared my room with Ma and got all the news from home as we talked long into the nights.

I met another figure from my past once when the coastal boat came north, a patient was brought from St. Anthony who had surgery on both legs and was in a cast from the waist down. He was a boy that I had gone to school with at Muddy Bay. This one patient's cast was a heavy burden on our nursing staff as it took two people to turn him. Many nights I was up with him several times. Often he was in pain and would need an injection. Sometimes there was an irritating itch somewhere under the cast, so I devised a scratcher with a clothes hanger

71

that could be pushed under the cast. There were times when I was so tired that when I'd hear his bell I would nearly cry. I had to bite my tongue so as not to say something sharp to him. One night as I finished giving him an injection and was settling him away for the night, he looked up at me and said, "Miss Blake, I often think about it." When I asked him what it was, he said, "I often think of how I burnt down the school and you and the others lost all your things and now you are so good to me." Then I was glad I had tried to be patient. This young man must have had this thing that he had done as a child on his conscience all these years.

There was little time for social life. Once the patients were cared for there was always so much to do; the daily clinics, the planning of meals, the supervising of kitchen and laundry staff, helping to bottle food for the winter, ordering supplies, making up and sterilizing dressings. In those days gauze and cotton wool came in bulk, and dressings were made by staff and patients, then sterilized, often by baking them in the oven.

As the days of summer sped quickly by I learned that a new nurse would be taking over at Cartwright and I would be sent to the main hospital at St. Anthony in the fall. The new nurse eventually arrived. She was older and more experienced than I, but knew nothing about Labrador and its people, so we had much valuable knowledge to pass on to each other. I helped her as much as I could to understand the people and their ways and to tell her of the IGA and its works. Days when we weren't too busy, I took her to meet some of the people and we took turns making house calls and shared night duty. In turn, she was able to give me the benefit of her nursing experience.

One day we heard a motorboat coming. A few minutes later I saw a fisherman hurrying up from the wharf carrying a child. As he handed her to me he told me she had been attacked by dogs earlier that day. He had left his fishing ground immediately to get her to the hospital. The child was in shock. She badly needed to be cleansed and stitched. What was I do to? Fortunately the new nurse was there so, while she cleansed and shaved the child's badly bitten scalp and arms, I scrubbed and prepared to sew up. The industrial worker came to help and acted as an anesthetist under our direction. Finally, we finished sewing and set up an intravenous drip. The girl was then placed in a cot which we had moved into my bedroom where she could be watched all night. It was an anxious few days and nights with little sleep, but gradually little Minnie improved and by the time the doctor arrived back from his trip north she was playing happily. Most of her wounds had healed and I was very pleased.

One of the patients that summer was a first cousin of mine who was about two years old, the darling of the hospital. He was being treated for osteomyelitis, a disease of the bones. I cuddled him and got comfort from him. That little boy often gave me the courage to go on, for sometimes I felt inadequate and knew I needed much more experience and knowledge if I was to be responsible for the welfare of such as he.

When Dr. Forsythe arrived back from his medical trip, he brought patients with him and we were very busy. Minor surgery was done in Cartwright those days and, with only one nurse, it put a great burden on her.

Eventually, I got my orders to proceed to St. Anthony. I asked if I might go home for a short visit, since I was so close to home. I particularly wanted to see my grandmother Oliver who was now an invalid. I was given a few days if I could find a way. I went from Cartwright to Rigolet on the Newfoundland Rangers' boat and spent a couple of very happy days at home looking after my grandmother. Then I got a chance to get to North West River to spend a few days seeing my friends and relatives. I visited the dear little hospital I dreamed of nursing in. In October I joined the coastal boat for my trip to St. Anthony.

When I arrived in St. Anthony I was met by one of the staff who took me to the Director of Nursing for introduction and instruction. I needed no introduction, for the Director was the same Miss Carlson that had been there when I was a child, but I found that she had much to teach me.

St. Anthony hospital was the only hospital on the northern coast of Newfoundland and Labrador for acute care, so it was always busy. My first tour of duty was in the small nursery and the male TB wards. We worked very hard and long hours. Sometimes there would be a weekend off, but off-time depended on the demands of the patients. A lot of babies were born at home, so in addition to the care of the babies in the hospital we would sometimes have to visit the homes. The Wops, medical students, future nurses and specialists who spent each summer working long hours with the regular staff played a large part in structuring the good reputation enjoyed by IGA at St. Anthony. They were sadly missed when they returned home in the fall.

Not long after I arrived at St. Anthony the last boat for the season departed and I found myself practically as far from home as I had been in the United States. There were no planes and no roads, and no boats could cross the Strait of Belle Isle in the winter. However, I knew many of the locals from my school days, so I soon found old friends and made new ones. That first winter I worked hard. I was the newest nurse there and I hoped I could contribute as much to the care of the patients as the others. We all worked well together. Usually there were a lot of tubercular patients who were brought to the hospital in the fall from the annex where they had been housed all summer. There we had three nurses, so two worked days and one worked on nights.

At that time, Dr. Charles S. Curtis was the Chief of Staff at St. Anthony and the head of the Grenfell Mission in Newfoundland and Labrador. At first I thought he was a very stern, sharp-spoken man. I didn't want to invite his anger, so I worked very hard to please him. Later we became good friends and worked well together. He trusted me and taught me a great deal. Once my fear of Dr. Curtis went away I would have worked for him for nothing out of friendship and respect.

My first tour of night duty came soon after I arrived. There were also two aides in the hospital and one on duty in the annex. The Mission had electric lights which were put off at ten o'clock each night and would stay off unless there was an emergency operation. We used lamps and flashlights on the wards, so every few hours the nurse had to light her lantern and make rounds over in the annex. I liked night duty. You were responsible for your patients and staff and for planning your own work. We ate together in the patients' waiting room, the aides, the night watchman and myself. When the wards were done and the patients sleeping, there were always dressings to make, cleaning of cupboards and utility rooms to be done, and a baby to cuddle. We learned to organize things so nothing was left over for the day shift. A month of nights flew quickly by and then you were back on days.

Although the hospital was quieter in the winter than during the summer rush, it was just as busy for the few staff that were there as it was when the full summer staff was on. Two doctors, three nurses and the Director of Nursing was the full medical staff for the winter, just enough to cover the wards. As soon as a nurse arrived she was taught and groomed for duty as a station nurse. I often felt, that first year, that I was being watched and judged so that the Mission could determine whether I had what it took to run a remote nursing station by myself.

I learned a great deal that first year in St. Anthony, and went to bed every night with a feeling of eager anticipation for the next day.

Each day I was learning things that only doctors did in hospitals like St. Luke's in Duluth, that a station nurse would probably have to do herself some day. Once, that first winter, a premature baby was born and I was responsible for looking after him. We had an old-fashioned incubator. It had to be heated by hot-water bottles and the only way to give oxygen then was directly from the tank. It was a major effort to care for premature babies with the equipment that was available. What a feeling of accomplishment, though, when the baby thrived! Many, many hours of overtime, day and night were spent with that baby. It was all worthwhile. Today he is a big strapping man with a family of his own.

It was the days when pneumothorax (inserting air into the lung cavity, so that the lung collapsed) was the treatment for tuberculosis. There was a day set aside when the annex patients were brought to the hospital on stretchers and carried back again. Being strong and healthy, I often found myself at one end of the stretcher while the doctor carried the other. We moved men and women back and forth. I watched first as the machinery was set up and then air was pumped into the chest. Soon I was doing it under the doctor's careful eye, then I took my turn with the other nurses if the doctors were unavoidably absent.

Some days were spent with the dentist who would teach as he gave injections, extracted teeth or put in temporary fillings. Then under his supervision we would do the injections and extractions. Every day the nurses took turns in the clinic, where the doctors taught us as they worked. We would examine a patient, make a diagnosis and suggest treatment. The doctor would examine the patient and either commend or correct.

There were medical trips as well for both doctors and nurses, which made it busier still for those who remained at the hospital. That first year I didn't go on a medical trip. I think it was because I probably needed more experience, which I hoped to get before the next season.

Once navigation opened in the spring the hospital at St. Anthony got busier still. The townspeople volunteered to do the housecleaning and everyone helped. After getting the patients cared for, we would join in and help. It was great fun and everyone had a good time. As far as I know, the only payment these women got or wanted was their meals and cups of tea. Miss Carlson made sure the meals were special and that there were good things to eat with the tea breaks. One day every week the mending for the hospital was done by those same women who volunteered their services.

One of the jobs given to me that first spring was to prepare the dispensary of the hospital ship, the *Maraval*, for the summer's travel. This was a most important job and I intended to give it my best. The boat had to be prepared for every eventuality, with medications for all things, maternity packs, suture trays and emergency appendectomy packs. Then there was a small dental clinic on the boat and its needs must also be met. All had to be set up, sterilized at the last possible moment and stored in the correct positions in the cupboards. It took weeks, since this task had to be fitted in with all the other work. Just before the boat sailed, the Chief of Staff would check everything over to make sure it was in order. Eventually it was all finished and the ship steamed away. It would go south first and on the way north it would come in for replenishments. This work soon became routine.

Summers at St. Anthony were one constant mad rush. Sometimes several boats would come in on the same day and many patients would be packed into the waiting room. Our routine was that one nurse would talk to the patient getting his or her history, make a tentative diagnosis and give the patient a slip of paper that would be handed to the doctor in the examining room. The doctor would then go over the patient and decide to admit, treat on the spot or send him or her to the annex. Another nurse directed the people where to go and assisted the doctor with his work. Many times we ended up with extra beds in halls, waiting rooms and any other available space. Very often we worked late into the night. One day when several boats came in and other people from nearby settlements came, we saw more than a hundred patients.

Some evenings it would be very late when we got back to caring for in-patients, but no matter how late it was we had to make sure they all had their treatments, medication and were settled away for the night. One night, very late when I was just about exhausted, I was preparing a patient for bed with the help of an aide. The radio was on farther down the hall and this voice was going on and on. Finally I couldn't stand it any longer so I shouted down the hall, "Would somebody please choke that odious man."

The aide said in a horrified voice, "Miss Blake, I'll have you know you're talking about my uncle."

I told her if I had an uncle like that I would go behind the house and shoot myself. After a good night's rest, we laughed about that. Today I would be proud to shake the hand of the man that was talking. It was the future Premier, Joseph R. Smallwood, whom I have admired for many years and whose program *The Barrel Man* was extremely popular at that time.

Some evenings there would be time to have a ballgame with the town girls in a field just off from the hospital, or we might get a chance to go out jigging cod with some fishermen. But, on the whole, summers were mostly hard work and I loved it all.

The Mission preferred staff to take their holidays in the fall or during winter. The Mission might arrange a trip on the IGA supply boat, *George B. Cluett* from St. Anthony to Charlottetown, Prince Edward Island, then back when the *Cluett* returned with the winter supplies. Although the only holiday I wanted was a trip to Labrador, summers were so busy it just wasn't the time to ask for leave.

That fall Dr. Curtis asked me to take over the operating room work and obstetrics. I was very pleased. The only trained midwife we had was leaving, so I took a crash course in practical obstetrics from her, helping with her clinics and deliveries. From then on, I did all the normal deliveries and assisted the doctor with more difficult births. Dr. Curtis did all the Caesarian sections and talked as he worked, explaining and teaching all of us, medical students, doctors and nurses. I was to spend the next two years as an O.R. nurse, a task that gave me tremendous satisfaction.

In those days we scarcely saw any specialists with the Grenfell Mission, except for volunteers during the summer. We were very lucky indeed that we had Dr. Curtis as Chief Surgeon and Chief of Staff. He was a doctor of great capabilities who seemed to be able to tackle any kind of surgery. He was always available, day or night. He was a stern and demanding taskmaster who expected of his staff the same dedication that he himself gave to duty.

Being an operating nurse and obstetrical nurse meant that in addition to all duties in the O.R. or delivery room you also made ready all supplies, solutions, local anesthetics and prepared all surgical packages. There was a sort of "recipe book" for all the solutions and a surgical package list for all types of operations. It was a formidable task at first, as all things had to be calculated with great care. Sometimes I worried about the effectiveness of the local anesthetics. Once, before an eye operation, I made up a new batch of local anesthetic that I was not sure about. I put a drop in my eye and in a little while I was able to prod and poke at my eye without experiencing any pain. Anesthesia for dentistry always bothered me. I remembered hearing my brother speak of the time he had a tooth extracted without an anesthetic. I hoped that those I made up would always be effective.

My days began early. Because time was always so full, I would get up and walk out to Fishing Point and back every morning. It was a quiet and beautiful time of the day. The fishermen would be getting

77

ready to go to their cod traps, smoke was beginning to rise from the stovepipes and the sun would be coming up over the horizon. The air was so clear and sweet. While I walked I planned my work for the day.

Operations began at eight and sometimes all day would be spent in the operating room. We broke for dinner, especially in the summer, but more often the operations would be over by noon. The afternoons would be spent scrubbing, cleaning, sterilizing and preparing for the next day's cases. Sometimes there would be an emergency operation during the night, and quite often I would be called to deliver a baby, which I did on my own, unless there were complications.

During the years I spent in the operating room, I had many interesting and sometimes frightening experiences. Once I was sent by dog-team to attend a delivery that a local midwife was worried about. Arriving at the home I found the baby could not be born without surgical intervention. I had to get the patient back to the hospital, and what a trip that was! It took about six hours. The patient travelled in a komatik box on one team, I travelled on another and the third team was sent ahead to notify the hospital that we were coming. What an anxious night! Every half hour we stopped while I checked the patient by flashlight. My only hope was that the third team would get through to the hospital. We arrived in the wee hours of the morning to see the hospital lights on. I was met by Dr. Curtis who said, "Get dressed, Blake. The O.R. is ready."

Because it was necessary to do trepanning, the baby died but the mother survived. During the operation Dr. Curtis looked up at me and said, "You certainly made the right decision that time, Blake. You could never have handled this one alone."

Another time a man fell across a saw and was badly injured. In the operating room Dr. Curtis removed several feet of bowel, tied off bleeders and stitched other wounds. The man weathered the operation and I specialled him day and night until it was evident that he would live.

We were more than tired sometimes, but Dr. Curtis' "Well done" made up for it all.

There were times I'd be in the operating room, standing ready for surgery, when Dr. Curtis would appear and motion for me to open the window. "Isn't it a wonderful morning. Look at those beautiful flowers. The air is so good." He was just bursting with the love of life and had to say it to someone.

There were emergency trips to the barn to help Dr. Curtis deliver a calf or treat a sick cow, for in those days the Mission kept cattle for milk and meat. There were gardens to supply most of the vegetables. Dr. Curtis had a profound interest in agriculture and husbandry. One of his accomplishments was the provision of a community garden and the giving of his knowledge and expertise to the people who had plots.

At that time I was the only nurse from either Newfoundland or Labrador with the IGA. The other nurses and the doctors were all Americans, for there were few English people with the Grenfell mission during the war. Sometimes it struck me how differently I was treated by the "outsiders" now that I was considered staff, while some of my relatives or friends were looked down upon. I soon concluded that the Mission was missing a golden opportunity by sticking to their own group. As staff I was treated well by the Mission and the doctors and nurses all tried to help me succeed. But, generally, the IGA did not make the most of their opportunities to educate the people about health matters. By this I do not mean that every child should have been given the opportunities for training that I had. Rather, I felt that the people of Newfoundland and Labrador were quite capable of putting to good use some basic information about such things as proper diet or home care if the importance of these matters was explained in layman's language, rather than medical terms.

I had many friends in town so I spent much of my time off with them. But, as surely as I was enjoying a dance, I would be called for an emergency. Christmas Eve we planned a party at Dr. Curtis' house, and my donation was a bottle of absinthe, a kind of liqueur that had been given to me by a Portuguese sailor patient. I had carefully kept it intact for Christmas. That evening we were called together because of a sudden emergency at the Orphanage. The children had been coming down with the measles and some were pretty ill, and the staff were worn out. The head nurse asked for a volunteer to go and stay over Christmas Eve night. One nurse was on night duty, one was on days, so that left me to volunteer. While I spent the night going from bed to bed and crib to crib, sponging down and forcing fluids, the rest of the staff had their party and forced down my absinthe. They refilled the bottle with water as a joke on me, but I laughed the loudest.

On special days all the staff found time to do things to cheer the patients as well. At Christmas time we made all the decorations, sometimes right on the wards with the patients helping us. All our wreaths were made of spruce boughs decorated with wool and popcorn. Each patient would get a gift, which most often came from the clothing store. One of us would dress up as Santa and pass out gifts on the wards and on Christmas morning the trays would be made specially attractive. Nurses, staff and visitors attended the church services put on in the wards.

Following the merry Christmas season, depression and boredom set in among the TB patients who had to rest in bed for months and months. What could be done to allay this boredom? Some of them couldn't read. We had a meeting and I suggested that we teach them how to knit. It was an easy and relaxing activity. Everyone thought it was a crazy idea, but we decided to give it a try. We made some money, bought some wool and needles and began our lessons. At first the men looked sheepish and if anyone came to visit they quickly hid their work under the blankets. However, before long you would walk into the ward and everyone was studiously busy, counting purls and plains. There were beautiful things produced — sweaters, caps, mitts, socks and so on. I was pleased to see the nurses learning along with the patients.

In the spring we had a sale of the goods and with the money earned we were able to buy more supplies for the patients. This proved to be really good occupational therapy. The patients were interested in other kinds of handiwork as well. One man knit fishnets, another lay propped up with pillows as he repaired watches. Watches soon came, not only from St. Anthony, but from outlying areas, so he was soon earning a small income. Having something to do surely made the patients more content.

Since this was during the war, sometimes a navy ship would come into the harbour. Once there was a flotilla of Welsh ships there. They looked like old wrecks. We found out that they had been picked up at Halifax and were being convoyed to England for war service. All the staff was invited aboard for a very good meal and a movie. The next day the nurses got an invitation from the officers to attend a dance in the town hall that night. We had a good time but I guess I stood out again since I danced most of the night with the fireman of the ship, rather than with the officer who was my escort. That fireman was certainly a talented dancer. All the jiving and twirling were just about right for our "Gone With the Wind" style dresses which were very much in vogue that year.

Another time that the war upset our routine was one summer morning when I was awakened by an aide and was informed that I was to get dressed immediately and prepare to go on the hospital ship *Maraval*. Dr. Curtis was waiting below. On the way to the ship he informed me that a telegram had come from the nurse in Forteau saying she had a sailor who had an accident. I'll never forget that trip, because on our way we came upon flotsam and jetsam in the ocean, which led us to believe we had a major shipwreck on our hands, but no sign of any boats. On docking in Forteau it was obvious that some disaster had taken place. Men were lying or sitting about on the rocks and the gravel in shirt-sleeves, some in pyjamas, many looked sick and many looked shocked. They told us that three boats of a convoy had been torpedoed there that morning. The nurse was trying to cope with those who had been injured. They were lying around on the floor of the small clinic. We all set to work doing what we could. Extra help was called in to help prepare meals, wash clothes and comfort the men. There was oil everywhere. All day we sorted out the sickest sailors. Our ship was small but we were able to carry back the six who needed hospital care most. Already word had gone out to the authorities about the remaining men. The men who came with us were terrified and we had a job to persuade them to get aboard. I stood by the side of the sickest man and held his hand all the way across the Straits. We had given him sedation so that he dozed off and on all the way across, waking with a start and terror in his eyes at the slightest motion of the waves.

As soon as we landed at St. Anthony, people came to meet us, telling us that bodies were being picked up along the coast and were being brought to the hospital morgue. All the staff pitched in to do what they could for the men. Some soon recovered, but one man died in spite of all that was done for him, he had so much oil in his lungs and stomach.

It was only then that the implications of war were really brought home to me. War always happened somewhere else, but now, suddenly, it was happening right outside our door. Those young men lying in the morgue had been deliberately killed in our own land. I thought of the rumours that had been going around St. Anthony for a while now. Just before this, during the summer in the small settlements, it was said that people had seen what looked like a boat of some kind suddenly appear on the shoreline. Some people said that greens had been taken from their gardens. Another small community said the same things. These rumours were said by the staff to be the imagination of the locals, brought on by similar stories on radio. Years later we began to find out that there was indeed some enemy activity on the coast of Labrador and northern Newfoundland.

11. *My first station alone, at Mary's Harbour.*

CHAPTER SIX

Station Nurse

In my first year at St. Anthony I made a medical trip along the Straits Coast. My driver was a man by the name of Reardon from Goose Cove, a small settlement just outside St. Anthony. We started off early on a morning after a snowstorm. The world looked beautiful, white snow everywhere with not a track in it. We had not travelled far along the hills when, suddenly, I found myself flying through the air. We landed in a flurry of snow on a ledge farther down the hill — dogs, komatik, driver and me, all in different places. I heard a cry of, "Miss, Miss, are you all right?" The driver was coming toward me at a run, face, hair and clothes all covered with snow. I was lying there too weak with laughter to get up. It struck me so funny — dogs landing everywhere and the driver disappearing in a snowbank. Looking up we saw how the snow hung over the cliffs. It was difficult to see where the edge really was.

It took all morning to get across one bay, stopping only once to boil up and have a lunch. We would stop in a tilt overnight and the next day house visits would begin. Late that afternoon we crossed a small bay when suddenly I noticed the motions of the komatik were different. Looking behind I could see the ice moving in a wave-like motion, what is known as "rubber ice". I had been on ice like this before. It is not frozen, but it is very thick and tough and there is no danger of falling through as long as you keep moving.

It was almost dark when we reached the tilt, hidden in a grove of trees. We dug our way in and soon had a fire going in the drum stove. While the driver fed the dogs, brought in the traces to dry and gathered wood for the night, I prepared our supper. One dog spent the night in the tilt with us because she was pregnant.

Next morning, looking out through the tilt doorway, we couldn't see any dogs at first. Another night of snow had covered them all with a warm blanket. We travelled along stopping at each little place while

I talked with the people, examined some, pulled a tooth or so, gave advice on some condition or other, passed out medications and made arrangements for hospitalization if necessary. As soon as we arrived at a house there would be a bustle, "Come in, Miss. Sam, pull up that chair by the stove for the nurse and open the oven door. John, bring in more wood. Mary, put the kettle on. Here, Miss, let me pull off your boots." The nurse usually ate alone. The driver would tend to the dogs and then have a cup of tea and yarn with the men of the house. I felt like an outsider, eating off by myself.

While I saw patients, the driver mended the harnesses, fixed the komatik and prepared for the next day. The driver knew where to stay, for there were certain places where the Mission people always stayed over the years. The first house we stayed at seemed to set a pattern which we were expected to follow. While we got warmed up at the kitchen stove there was a bustle of activity around the house and we would smell a meal being prepared. Sometimes it would be salt fish, or rabbits, or seal meat. I would sit there practically drooling. When it was time to eat, the woman of the house would take me to the inside part of the house where a table was covered with a linen cloth. These were the best dishes she had, and there might be canned meat, pickles and tinned fruit. While I ate alone (and I longed to be with the family) they ate rabbit, jam and bread. I would have enjoyed it so much if I could have joined with them in the talking and laughing. At first I thought that perhaps I should be keeping up appearances, but I soon made it known that I did not want this preferential treatment. I was one of them. I had grown up and lived the way they did. I was not only more comfortable eating with the family, but it made good professional sense as well. Joining the family and sharing their meals was an opportunity to learn. The things I learned helped me in my evaluation of their medical needs. In this manner I made valued friends and respected them, and I believe I kept the respect and co-operation of the people.

One stop on that first trip was a night on the coastline. Looking out over the Strait I could see the outline of Labrador. The men of the house had begun sealing, so I decided to take the morning off and go with them. Before daylight we started walking toward the edge of the ice. It was rough going; sharp edges of the ice could be felt through our skin boots. We had to climb over pinnacles and there were places where the men would have to push ice pans apart and we had to jump over the water. Just before the sun came up, we reached the edge of the ice. Ice pans floating by sometimes grazed the ice we stood on.

Once a large pan came by, just out of reach. It was full of seals. The whitecoats looked at us with huge brown eyes. The pan was just out of jumping distance and couldn't be reached with the gaff to haul it nearer. Secretly I was glad. I knew that soon there would be a pan that the men could reach and that every day, while the season lasted, men would be out getting seals. This was part of the livelihood of our people. No part of the seal was wasted; we ate the meat, clothed ourselves with the skins, and the blubber was used in preparing the dogs' feed and sometimes rendered and sold for commercial purposes. On the way in from the ice edge, the sun was high and it got very warm. I got very thirsty so I was going to eat some ice. Then, off in the distance, we saw a couple of small dots. One of the men said, "Here come the kids with some tea." The tea was cold but I had never before tasted anything so good.

Whenever we left a house we had some addition to our bread box — a loaf of fresh bread, some frozen baked beans or a piece of seal. People were so pleased to be able to give something. We were always given the best they had and they often did without themselves in order to give us something for our journey.

We continued our trip, stopping at all the homes, and wherever there was a cluster of houses I'd hold a clinic. It was a busy time and a very enjoyable one. There was time to yarn with the older people, time to spend with the children, time to teach as I went, and so a link was forged between the people and the Mission that helped to promote mutual respect and co-operation. Many of the people that were visited would, no doubt, come to the hospital at some time and this contact would lessen some of the anxiety people feel about leaving home and going to a hospital.

The war was still on and it was getting a bit harder for the Mission to hire staff, especially doctors. There was one woman doctor with IGA at that time, an American stationed at Mary's Harbour in southern Labrador. She had been called up for service and was leaving, as was the nurse there. Dr. Curtis asked me if I would care to take on the station. It was quite a difficult decision to make. I was happy at St. Anthony, but I also felt I would like to run a station on my own. Dr. Curtis said that he felt I was ready. He gave me this advice: "Do your best, Blake, and give it your all. The Mission will always back you up."

It was with a feeling of sadness mixed with eager anticipation, that I left St. Anthony, going on the northbound trip of the *Kyle*, late in the summer of 1943. I was surprised at the number of passengers who were afraid to go below to sleep that night for fear that we would be torpedoed. I felt as safe on the *Kyle* as I had when I was a girl, going to the school at St. Anthony.

At Mary's Harbour I was met by the doctor and nurse who would soon be leaving. My first impression of Mary's Harbour was of a quiet, beautiful, clean, green piece of home. Friendly faces smiled as I climbed up onto the tiny wharf. Not far away was a neat three-story building, larger than all the others. This was the hospital and I was immediately enchanted with it. While the doctor went off to see to her goats, the nurse showed me around and introduced me to the staff. The little hospital seemed pleasant, compact and efficient. On the Mothers' Ward there were two mothers and their babies. I noticed the babies had gauze spread over the tops of their cribs and you couldn't see their faces. When I asked why it was there, the nurse said it was to keep the dust off. I thought this was a strange practice and poor stimulation for the babies. I made a mental note to let the babies see more of their surroundings. Following the tour, we went for supper in the staff quarters. The doctor arrived and brought with her such an odor of goat that I could scarcely eat. She was a great believer in goats' milk for her patients, especially the TB patients, who drank the milk under protest, never having been used to milk of any kind.

I heard more about the goats at supper, with instructions on how to take care of them. The doctor said she'd been having trouble with people's dogs and would take me out to show me how to handle the problem. At one house there was a group of men standing about. She went up to one of them and gave him a verbal blast in front of all his friends. She threatened to shoot his dogs if they were ever left untied again. I stood behind her, dying of embarrassment, and smiled, winking at the man as much as to say, "Don't worry, she'll soon be gone. I don't treat people this way." I could tell he understood my actions. I can't judge that doctor, since I never really worked with her, because the few days I was with her she spent most of the time with her goats.

Soon I found myself alone again, but this time I knew that I had some help. Celeste Gerber, one of the nurses I had worked with formerly at St. Anthony was marrying a local man, so I would have her to call on in times of distress. That was a big help, but it did not change the fact that, for the first time, I would be completely responsible for the health care of a community and its surrounding areas. There was no doctor to call upon. I would only be able to reach a doctor if I sent a dog-team or boat to Battle Harbour, some seven miles away, where the nearest wireless station was. I was far too busy to worry about being alone.

In addition to the health care, I also ran the clothing store. All IGA stations had clothing stores, as I mentioned before. People in America, Canada and England would send second-hand clothing and other goods to be given to the people who needed them. Over the years it got to be quite a business. Local people would bring meat, fish, berries, hooked mats, locally-made boots and other things and in return would receive clothing. The Labrador people were clothed this way for many years, because the Hudson's Bay Company carried little manufactured clothing in those days apart from rubber boots, overalls, oilskins and underwear. The HBC did carry cloth and woolen goods. The people who could afford it bought these and made their own clothing.

Usually the clothing store would be open on scheduled days during the week. I would rise in the morning to see boats coming from all directions, often quite a crowd, because it was also an opportunity to come to the clinic. Many times it was very late in the day when I finally finished.

Certain days I spent with the school children, checking eyes, ears, heads and teeth. I also played with them. I visited people who were housebound and the seniors who didn't get out much.

Mary's Harbour was a small place and I soon knew everyone there. The people were friendly, kind, and very hospitable so I felt at home almost immediately. Not long after I arrived, Celeste's wedding took place. She did me the honour of asking me to be the Maid of Honour. I had some yards of material which I had intended to make into a robe. I used it to make my dress. It was a lovely wedding that was the beginning of a long and happy marriage. Gordon and Celeste Acreman brought up a family to be proud of. They still live in Mary's Harbour and they continue to be pillars of the community.

In my new position there was never a moment to spare. My staff consisted of a cook, a laundress, an aide, a chore boy and a maintenance man. I could not have managed without their help. Uncle Sam Acreman, the maintenance man, became my friend, my right hand and my mentor.

Sometimes I'd get a few hours to go up the lovely little river and have lunch in a little cabin with friends, go fishing or walk about in the beautiful woods and hills of St. Mary's River. Some evenings people would come to visit me. There would be tea, conversation and fellowship. Later in the year I spent many evenings skating alone on the ice just outside the hospital where I could be easily found. I never had a day off while I was there, but I never found that I needed one.

Once, late in the fall, a motorboat came for me from Fox Harbour. It was snowing and cold. A man had what sounded like a stroke and I needed to get to him. After going along for some time, the engine stopped. We started to drift far out from the land toward the open sea. It grew rougher and colder. Just as I was getting very worried, they got the engine to go and, eventually, cold and hungry, we arrived at our destination. I was always amazed at the skill of local men with engines. They were the best self-made mechanics I ever saw. Sometimes all they needed was a nail or a piece of wire.

It was necessary to take the patient back, so I insisted on having a tent on the boat and the use of a tent stove. We had it warm and cozy for the patient and ourselves on the way back. The patched engine never failed.

It was a busy fall. The weather was good and boats came constantly. Sometimes it was someone to have a tooth pulled, or someone who just wasn't well. I worked away, sometimes not knowing what was really wrong with the patient and always wishing I knew more. Before the boats stopped for the fall, I got some instructions from St. Anthony about new drugs or treatments and how I should use them for certain conditions. One such drug was sulfanilamide (the first of the antibiotic drugs that were to revolutionize medicine) You were supposed to give it every four hours, on time, or it would not be effective. This caused many, many restless nights later on in the winter.

Late in the fall a boat carried me up the narrow bay to Port Hope Simpson to see a patient. The hills were aflame in fall colours and the sun shone on the crystals of ice forming on the beaches. We passed little homes with their smoke going straight up into the cloudless sky. Peace and beauty were all around us. All we could hear was the bark of a dog or a child's laughter as we passed the scattered houses. The beauty of the trip was a stark contrast to the hopelessness of the scene which awaited me. The woman I had come to see had a huge mass in her abdomen. She was very ill and I knew in my heart what was wrong, cancer. I had to call her husband aside and tell him that I could take her to the hospital, keep her comfortable and pain free, but I could do no more. The coastal boat had stopped running for the year and there was no way to get her to St. Anthony. In any case, Mary's Harbour was a better place for this patient. Her husband could come to see her whenever he wished and until freeze-up he came to see her often. She eventually died and was taken home for burial on the first ice.

Just after freeze-up a team brought in a young woman in labour. I had never met her before. She had been in labour for some time and the local midwife had been unable to deliver her. No wonder! On examination I could hear no heartbeat from the baby and the woman had TB and was extremely ill. The birth passage was very small. I told her husband to stay, as I felt the woman would not live. Celeste came and administered the anesthetic for me while I delivered a large dead baby with forceps. We could no nothing more than keep the mother comfortable until her death a few hours later. I agonized over this. I wondered why I had put myself in this position. How dared I think that I had knowledge enough to be in charge of people's lives! I didn't really believe that she could have been saved, but I yearned to have Dr. Curtis with me, if only to have someone to talk to about my fears.

Not long after that another young woman came in by dog-team, already in difficult labour. After examining her I sent a dog-team flying to Battle Harbour to send a telegram to St. Anthony asking for advice. After waiting some hours the driver came back with the news that it was useless to send a message as the reception was bad. No one would have been able to get from St. Anthony anyway. So, taking myself in hand, I got Celeste to come and give anesthetic while I delivered another forceps baby. Happily, mother and baby did well.

After these two difficult births I noticed a pattern in the way that I would respond to a crisis. While the patient was in danger I would become almost another person, letting my training take over. It was only later that, alone in my room, I would find that self-doubt crept in and my knees would shake for hours.

The little hospital was never empty. We always had the TB ward full of patients who had come back from St. Anthony in the fall to spend the winter on bed rest. There were always mothers and babies (in those days we kept the mothers in bed ten days or so after giving birth). And then we had Mr. Doane. He had been in hospital for some time with ulcers. As is often the case with a resident patient, this situation benefitted me, as Mr. Doane made it his business to "nurse the nurse". He always made sure I was dressed properly, as if I didn't know how. He always got up and made a hot fire when I was expected back from a trip. He made skin boots for me, was always at my elbow to help when I returned from a dog-team trip cold and hungry. He always had a comfortable chair drawn up to the fire where he would sit me down and haul off my boots and give me a hot toddy, wherever he got it. Sometimes I wondered who was the nurse and who was the patient. The conversations we had! He was a most interesting man. Once he crossed the Strait of Belle Isle with the mail in the winter. He walked, hauling his canoe on a komatik, paddling over any water and then getting back on the ice again. Sometimes Mr. Doane would cook something special for all of us, and his ideas for decorating come Christmas and Easter were the best. He made pictures using sealskin, local mosses, plants and trees. A special one hung in the little staff living room. I certainly valued his friendship that winter.

That Christmas we made our decorations and did up the wards in our little hospital as best we could. I decided we would hold an open house on Christmas Eve. For days before this, Lizzie, the cook, was very busy, happily cooking cakes, cookies and pies. My contribution was to make spruce beer. I had often seen my father make it so I knew what to do. Some of the local boys could play guitar. We sang, danced and drank our beer into the wee hours of Christmas Day. It was the highlight of our winter social season!

Just after Boxing Day the Newfoundland Ranger came to make it known to me that making beer was breaking the law. Being a decent sort he let me off, luckily for me. The law against beer-making was one thing (and in the case of my spruce beer I'm sure the alcohol content was very low), but there was also an unwritten law that no alcoholic beverage was ever allowed in a Mission building.

Earlier, during late fall, I went to Battle Harbour to see my patients there and in the surrounding area. At Battle Harbour I met a gentleman who managed a business buying fish and outfitting fishermen for Baine Johnston and Company. Sidney Loder was a Newfoundlander who first came to Labrador as a fisherman but, being "a good scholar and a poor sailor", he had soon found work in the fishery supply business. As the fall and winter progressed we met several times and became interested in each other. Soon I would get a note or a case of chocolate bars each time a team would arrive. It just so happened that when I got a call to go to Port Hope Simpson where a flu epidemic was raging Sid was the first person I met on arrival. He, too, was there on business. I found a lot of very ill people. I spent the days going from house to house fighting fever and pain. Now was the time to use the sulfanilamide, so I went to each house every four hours. I could trust no one else to administer this drug. I didn't mind the daytime, when the dogs were usually away from the community, but during darkness they were all around. I don't know how I would have managed if Sid hadn't been there with a stick to guard me as we went from house to house. I stayed at Port Hope Simpson until I knew the people were on the road to recovery, then I returned to the hospital.

Once that spring, a friend of mine came to have her baby. We had gone to school together; now she was married and had a large family. I delivered her easily, made her comfortable and, leaving her in the care of the aide, I went for a much-needed sleep. Soon I was awakened by the aide telling me that something was wrong with the patient. I found that she was hemorrhaging. While I worked over her, scenes flashed through my mind of having to send a team to inform her family that she had bled to death. Finally, ever so slowly, following drugs and manipulation, she started to respond. I spent the rest of the night and well into the next day by her bedside. I was afraid to leave her. There was nothing to do only hope that the bleeding didn't recur. Once again I remained calm during the crisis, only to be overcome by exhaustion later, my knees shaking. She went home some time later with strict instructions from me that if she had another baby to have it in the hospital.

Once a young man came with a heavily-bandaged hand. On examination I found it to be hot, red and infected. After some days the infection started to subside and there, at the tip of his finger, was the exposed bone. There was nothing to do but remove the fingertip and save it to show the doctor. The infection cleared up quickly after that.

My best-remembered dog-team trip came one stormy night. Luckily the weather turned mild and we had to go only three miles through the storm. The father of the driver had collapsed. There were three of us since it was necessary to have a third man going ahead with a flashlight. Eventually we arrived and I was sure my patient had suffered an acute heart attack. There was nothing to do except keep him comfortable, instruct the family and make it known to them that he probably would not survive very long. I was very exhausted when I finally sank into the middle of the feather bed. You haven't lived until you have slept in a feather bed. The warmth and comfort it always provided was unsurpassed. I stayed a few days until my patient stabilized and then went back to the hospital.

I had one patient who attended most clinics. He complained of pain in his upper arm, but I couldn't find anything wrong with it. I kept him happy by changing his rubbing ointments. We had many long and interesting conversations and sometimes he would stay for a meal. I decided his arm was more or less an excuse to visit and talk. Then one day, just after I said good-bye to him, the aide came running and crying, "Miss Blake, come quick. Mr. Pye is after falling off his komatik and he's hurt his arm." Sure enough, the crunch of the bone was unmistakable. So, while Uncle Sam held the arm in position I applied a plaster cast. I watched over him all night to see if circulation was good and he was without pain, then I discharged him. I was afraid to remove the cast when the time came, so I left it until the doctor's visit some weeks later. When the cast was removed, although the arm was stiff from being in the one position so long, it was well-healed and normal. What a relief!

Dr. Spicer's visit was the major event of the winter season. He travelled from Cartwright to Battle Harbour by dog-team, visiting all the little communities along the way. When he arrived at Mary's Harbour I was ready for him. All patients needing to see him were told to come in when he arrived. I also saved as many of the patients needing extractions as I could, because I hated extracting teeth. Dr. Spicer sorted out the patients who needed to go to St. Anthony when the boats started. He gave me instructions on how to care for them, brought the medicines and supplies that I could use and, above all, gave me comfort and boosted my confidence when I related to him my fears of being inadequate. After he attended to the patients in Mary's Harbour, we travelled together to the outlying communities of my district. In the evenings he told me all the news from along the coast and in St. Anthony. The time flew. It was just like having a holiday to have someone who could take over the responsibilities for a few days. As I waved good-bye to him, I knew he was the last doctor I would see until open water when the boats started running again.

Not long after the doctor left, our laundress, a lady over sixty, fell downstairs and broke her thigh bone. I put her to bed and applied a Thomas splint and prayed she'd be all right. So our workload increased a little. We all helped to do the laundry and the ironing. Soon Aunt Patience felt well enough to do all the mending and could peel vegetables for the cook, or knit socks for the TB patients. Nearly every day I had a cup of tea with her in her room. Since putting on the splints and weights she had felt comfortable. I could do no more so I left her there until she was able to go to St. Anthony on the first boat. When an X-ray was taken she was found to have had a fracture but it had healed perfectly.

Winter was passing quickly and I was kept busy. Sometimes it would be a pet that needed attention. One day Celeste brought in her cat which had broken its leg. First we put the cat in a bag to anesthetize it, then we manipulated and applied a cast. It was funny to watch the cat when she awakened. She tried to shake off the cast, licked it, and finally got used to it. She spent much of her time under the stove where it was warm so the cast dried quickly, and she thumped around on it until she was healed.

Sid and I had all winter to think about our feelings for each other and that spring we became engaged. I didn't feel so alone anymore. Although we could only see each other on occasional weekends, I had someone kind and wise to talk to.

We decided on an early wedding, in order to get married and settled during the summer. At this time the government was taking over many of the northern posts from the Hudson's Bay Company. Sid had applied for a government job and was accepted as depot manager in Hopedale, so that was where we would live. I wrote my letter of resignation to IGA and looked forward to the summer with eager anticipation. We got together as often as possible and talked about our plans.

12. The hospital at St. Anthony.

CHAPTER SEVEN

Volunteer Midwife

As my time at Mary's Harbour drew to an end I felt some sadness about leaving. I had made good friends among the people there and we had weathered numerous storms with their health. I felt that I had learned a lot as a nurse and as a person; certainly I had matured. I knew that Mary's Harbour would always hold a special place in my heart for, along with everything else, it was through that posting that I had met the man with whom I hoped to share the rest of my life. As well as the sadness I felt as I waved good-bye, in the spring of 1943, I was filled with anticipation of our lives ahead.

Sid and I spent some time in St. John's fitting ourselves out, then took the first boat north to Hopedale. The trip north from St. John's to Hopedale took about ten days. It was a journey of delight, visiting all the little settlements along the way, as once again the *Kyle* provided me with an opportunity to revisit places and people which meant so much to me. The feeling of making a fresh start was overpowering on this trip, as this was the first boat of the year. It seemed that each place we stopped shared some of the excitement that Sid and I felt. At St. Anthony I was able to take my husband ashore to meet my friends at the IGA and show him off. Also at St. Anthony a nurse who had taught me much about obstetrics, my friend Hazel Compton, embarked on a much-needed break. As we sailed along I noticed that Hazel kept visiting the boat's mailman, yet I was surprised when she told me that they were getting married and asked if my husband and I would stand for them if the Captain would consent to marry them. So, one morning as we passed a little place called Independence, quite appropriate I thought, the Captain performed the marriage ceremony and we had a nice little celebration. (I ran into Hazel again a little while ago and was pleased to see that she had the same enthusiasm that characterized her work with the Mission. Several of her children were making careers in the medical field.)

In Rigolet Sid and I went ashore for a few minutes, although it was the middle of the night, and for the first time the members of my family met my husband.

I had never been farther north than Rigolet, so the rest of the trip seemed even more like a wonderful new adventure. I found the northern coast much different from Hamilton Inlet and the southern coast. The cliff-and-rock formation was very impressive, but the vegetation was very scarce and houses clung to the rocks.

As we sailed into Hopedale it was dull and drizzly, not the best circumstances to see a new home for the first time. The houses were all a dull gray and seemed a part of the rocks on which they were built. There was one large, imposing building, the Moravian Mission premises. This was the building we were to live in.

Hopedale was to be my introduction to a part of Labrador that was new to me. It was almost entirely an Eskimo community (in those days we rarely used the word Inuit). I had grown up among Eskimo or part-Eskimo families, so that I had really not given much thought about whether I would find Hopedale to be any different. In Hopedale, however, there were no "settlers" who were a mixture of the two races: there were about 150 Eskimo people and there were the whites (Sid and I, a German-Dutch missionary couple, a teacher, the wireless operator and a Ranger.) Hopedale was one of the missions of the Moravian Church, a German congregation that had run missions to the Labrador Inuit since the late 1770s.

As the *Kyle*'s anchor rattled down boats circled the steamer, waiting to come aboard. As soon as I stepped ashore an Eskimo woman stepped up to ask me if I could see her daughter. So, before I saw where I was going to live, I went and found my first patient, a young woman who was badly injured during delivery. Of course it was necessary to get her to hospital, so I soon had her settled away aboard the *Kyle* and off to the nearest doctor — at Cartwright, 200 miles away.

Although I was no longer employed as a nurse, from the first it was clear to me that my experience as a nurse was needed at Hopedale. In the Moravian missions the missionaries took responsibility for the health of the community. Most of the missionaries, like Siegfried Hettasch at Hopedale, had some medical training and also had a great deal of practical experience, but the Moravians were glad of my help. They practiced homeopathic medicine (which involved giving patients small doses of drugs which would, in a healthy person, cause symptoms of the disease being treated), a tradition of which I knew nothing at all. I decided early on that my role would be to help out wherever

I could, whenever I was asked. Soon I was responsible for most of the work involving midwifery and I was very happy to be following in the footsteps of Ma, as a volunteer helping people to "find babies".

The Moravian mission at Hopedale was a long two-story building with a church at one end. The main part of the building was a long hall, there were rooms on either side. At the end of the hall was the part of the building where Sid and I were to live. The people that we were relieving left with the *Kyle*, so as I looked around I could scarcely wait to make a home for us. There was a kitchen, dining/living room, storage room, our bedroom and, off the bedroom, my husband's office. I remember that one of my first impressions was that I would have to change the colours, for everything was painted green and mustard. In the kitchen was a large, wood-burning stove with an attached water tank which held about two gallons of water. The rest of the house was heated by a large tile stove that nearly reached the ceiling. It was a beautiful thing that gave us much comfort. If filled with wood late at night and the drafts adjusted properly, there would be live coals until morning. While I appreciated the craftsmanship of the German-made stove, some of the other furnishings were very different from what I had been used to, being of German or Dutch make. The door handles in all the rooms, for instance, were very strange.

There was a flurry of activity as we arrived, for summers are very busy in the north. Fishermen moved out of the bays to settle on islands near their fishing grounds for the summer and every day there were boats coming and going. Some needed salt for curing their fish while others, perhaps, needed groceries. In the store, where Sid worked, there was no fresh meat, fruit (except occasional apples and oranges when the boat came in), or vegetables (except potatoes). The store did sell salt beef, salt pork and tinned food. From the country there was always plenty of fish and trout and you never lacked for fresh meat from birds and beasts of the land.

The coming of the coastal boat was always of great interest for it was the only link, apart from radio, that we had with the outside world. Everyone came in from the fishing grounds when they saw the boat coming, to hear the news and see if there was anything or anyone new. It was difficult to get things organized while the boats were running. Sometimes, I longed for the summer to pass and the boats to stop running so that I could get our quarters done for the winter and begin to explore the country around me. Hopedale was as far north as the *Kyle* went. Anyone going to Davis Inlet, Nain or Hebron had to go the rest of the way by small boat. Much of my time was taken up by cooking for and putting up travellers going along the coast, much as my mother had done during my childhood at Rigolet. It certainly felt that I was running a half-way house at times, but I met many nice people that way. By the end of the summer I certainly knew all the white people in the northern ports.

All that first summer I painted, made curtains and generally tried to make our living quarters more attractive. Gradually things began to take shape. Our social life was largely getting to know the few other whites in Hopedale. I practiced my cooking on our guests — and especially on the poor Ranger, who lived alone.

The Eskimo people of Hopedale were friendly and happy, with a very positive outlook on life and a great love for their children — two qualities that I have always looked for in those whom I would number among my friends. Their homes, which had struck me as dull upon my arrival, I soon found to be clean and inviting. Like most Labradorians, the people of Hopedale were delighted to have visitors and offered the best they had, so I was soon welcome in any home and my new friends were delighted to visit me as well.

We found as we got to know the people we began to appreciate the land around us more as well. Every Sunday, Sidney and I explored the hills and valleys around us and took little boat trips around to the islands and bays whenever it was possible. We grew to love the land and its special beauty.

Reverend Hettasch and I soon had a good working relationship. Whenever anyone was sick the missionary would discuss the case with me and we decided together what the treatment should be. Whenever someone came to me for medical help or advice I made sure they had gone to the missionary and had obtained his permission first. The mid-wifery was left for me and the local midwife. I remember well my first delivery in Hopedale. I was called in the wee hours of the morning (the time when so many babies seem to want to be born) and went with the father to his little one-room house. The children had been carted off to some neighbour's and there was a blazing fire in the stove. The mother was in labour and seemed to be doing quite well. When I asked for something to keep the bed clean, she pointed to a seal skin that had been washed just for this purpose. When I boiled up string and scissors and scrubbed my hands, she asked what I was doing and why. As she seemed interested, I thought I could teach as I worked, and I kept up this practise while I was in Hopedale.

When the boats stopped for the season, we settled down to a comfortable routine. Until the ice formed the men would be hunting whenever the waters were still enough, for the ducks were plentiful. Soon the back porch, which served as a refrigerator, was well stocked with ducks, geese, hares and partridge. I often saw companies of white partridges fly past the window and land on the rocks nearby. Fish, seal meat and local berries rounded out our well-balanced meals. Most of the vegetables, fruits and milk came in cans and had to be ordered each year, along with the eggs and cheese. I found it difficult at first to order a year's supply at a time. Eggs were preserved by putting them in water glass. They stayed fresh for a surprisingly long time. I often had a few left until fresh eggs could be gathered from the ducks' nests around the islands nearby.

The social highlight of our week, during the late fall and winter season, was Monday nights when we would get together with the missionaries, the teacher, the Ranger and the wireless operator and listen to the popular radio program of the time, "Lux Theatre". Later we'd have a cup of tea and yarn about the week's events.

My visits in the community also multiplied, so that I had several women and babies to look after and others who were making boots and parkas for my husband and me. I also was pregnant so I was busy knitting and sewing diapers and clothes for my baby. We were very happy together, Sidney and I, and we laughed all the time. I knew that I was in excellent condition and I did not worry about having my baby in isolation, for my confidence in the local midwife grew as she accompanied me on more and more deliveries.

Once, late in my pregnancy, I was called to a tiny home for a delivery. The bedroom had a low, slanted room which was papered with newspapers. While my patient napped, I kept reading the papers by the flickering lamplight. Next morning I was the one with the stiff neck and back and the mother and baby were great.

When my own labour started prematurely one cold winter's night, I had to make a quick decision. The midwife who would have delivered me was being treated for sore hands. I was afraid of infection, so I instructed my husband and we decided to deliver the baby ourselves. So when little David Blake Loder was born he was completely ours. He was tiny but strong and he thrived with loving care. David was a contented and happy baby and was easily trained into a routine that left me free to help the missionaries with medical problems.

During our second summer at Hopedale I received a letter from the wife of the superintendent of the Moravian Mission at Nain,

Reverend Peacock. Would I come and deliver her baby when her time came? I think I wrote that I would prefer that she to go the hospital at Cartwright, but she insisted on staying at Nain. In the end I took my own baby and embarked on the coastal boat for Nain.

What a fantastic trip we had! We called in at all the smaller places, and visited Davis Inlet, where the Indians camped up and down the coast at all the fishing places. We sailed up into a bay and there, under an impressive landscape, the community of Nain spread out. The mission building and the Hudson's Bay Company buildings were the largest and most efficient-looking places, while the small gray houses of the Eskimos clustered nearby.

At Nain the missionary and his wife were English. Rev. Peacock was the superintendent of the Labrador Moravian Missions and his wife was a well-qualified school teacher. She was a lovely and genteel lady, beloved by those around her. They both contributed a great deal to the welfare of the people of northern Labrador during their many years of service. I stayed in their home and I was made very welcome indeed. On examining my patient I found the baby was in the wrong position and I worried about this a great deal. One day a plane came and there was a young doctor on board. I told him of my worries and, after examining my patient, he looked down his nose at me and said I had nothing to worry about as everything was as it should be. I was much relieved, but the thought nagged at me that the baby's head was not where it should be at that stage in her pregnancy; also the doctor's attitude had shattered some of my confidence. When my patient went into labour I never left her side for I was still worried. Sure enough, when she was well into labour, I saw signs of a frank-breech position (which means that the baby was coming out feet-first). An older retired missionary, Siegfried's father, came to give me a hand and gave anesthetic under my instructions while, somehow, I managed to turn the baby and finally delivered a little blue girl. It took some time for the baby to start breathing and I don't know if the parents knew it or not, but I worried for years about their child, fearing that she might have brain damage. However, she turned out to be a bright intelligent child.

That fall a family stayed with us in Hopedale, waiting to get a boat back to Nain. Very soon, I noticed that the children had whooping cough and I knew my baby had been exposed. I worried some but knew that David was strong and healthy. Children don't usually die from whooping cough but from the complications of it, so I made sure to watch David very closely. I was so frightened when David did develop the cough. I spent much of the time, when the weather was good, carrying him around in my arms in the fresh air. Gradually he started to improve. Late that fall we were saddened to hear that the people who had gone to Nain with their sick children had lost one little boy and the other was left deaf from the complications of whooping cough.

The possibility of a real epidemic in Hopedale was always a major worry. One morning, after we had been in the community for some time, we were awakened about two or three in the morning by someone banging on the door. I woke to find a very worried-looking Reverend Hettasch. He told me that a boat had come from someplace near Davis Inlet, carrying a family whose children were ill. One child had died before they left home and one was in difficulty in the boat. When I asked what the symptoms were, he said, "Sore throat and fever."

I had a gut feeling that we were going to find diphtheria, a very catching disease that could be a real problem in those days. Covering our mouths and noses, we went to the wharf. Even before I looked down the sick girl's throat I felt that I knew what I would find : a dirty gray, wrinkled membrane, almost keeping her from breathing. She was whistling air through a tiny opening in her throat. We isolated the family in the school house. As soon as the wireless office opened in the morning we sent a message to the head of the Grenfell Mission's northern service at North West River, Dr. Tony Paddon. (Young Dr. Paddon was the son of Dr. Harry and Mina Paddon, who had been at North West River when I worked there.) Thank goodness Dr. Paddon took my word about the seriousness of the situation at Hopedale. An Air Force plane came and dropped a lot of vaccine and intravenous solution and took the girl back to North West River where the diagnosis was confirmed. Then our work really began.

No one was allowed in or out of Hopedale until the danger passed. Boats were not allowed to land, but had to anchor off shore; no one was permitted on shore and no one could go aboard. Reverend Hettasch and I had a monumental task. We had to inoculate every man, woman and child, as well as treat those who were already sick. We worked out a very good system. After working out the dosage, the missionary would draw up the serum and I did the injections. First we did the children, starting with my David who was four and a half. I explained how sick we would all get if he didn't take the treatment. I said to him, "Now David, you are a big brave boy, and I'm going to give you the first injection. When the other children see how good you are they'll know it doesn't hurt very much and they'll be good too."

So, we called all the children into the house and I did David first.

His face got very red and there were tears in his eyes but he smiled bravely and didn't let out a squeak. It took ages to do everyone, and it seemed a long time that we were isolated. It was all worthwhile because, apart from the family that came with the diphtheria, there was only one additional case, a girl whose mother insisted on visiting the sick family in the school house.

The children, however, responded well to treatment and we were very fortunate that there was no more spreading. Oh how I worried, about my own children as well as the others. Eventually, in late fall, we came off isolation.

Our David was christened by the Moravian missionary. I had started going to church there when we arrived. I found it quite strange at first for all the women and girls sat on one side of the church while the men and boys sat on the other side. The women wore little white church caps and always brought their babies with them. Whenever a baby would cry during the service the mother would breast-feed there in the church, which I thought was quite appropriate and actually added to the services. The music was beautiful. All the service and the singing was in Inuktituk, a language that I did not need to speak in order to appreciate the natural musical talent of the people.

The church, which adjoined the long mission building, was always kept clean and was much respected by all. In those days the whole community went to church. There were special celebrations for each category of the congregation. Young men and young women had their days, widowed and married people had their days, and so did the children. On their special day, all participants dressed in the best they had. They would decorate themselves with ribbons and broaches. They wore white silipaks (or parkas) and white-bottomed skin boots. The day was spent visiting homes, where they would be offered food and drink, and they would go to special church services. I thought this was a lovely custom so I tried to have cookies and syrup available for special days.

Christmas was also a special time. Church services went on all day. Each home had a Christmas tree (for the custom of Christmas trees had been brought to northern Labrador by the German missionaries long before it was common practice in Newfoundland) decorated with bits and pieces of homemade trinkets, shiny paper, red tinfoil from candy wrappers, home-made cookies, ribbon bows and small candles which were lit at night and carefully watched. Everyone hung up their stockings on Christmas Eve and again on Old Christmas Eve, January

5th. The gifts were much the same as I had received at home when I was a child, except that there was always a special gift of a toy for, like the IGA, the missionaries received barrels of clothing and toys from abroad to distribute to the people.

We, too, had a Christmas tree in the corner of our living room which we decorated with berries, popcorn and candles for our first Christmas. On Christmas Eve someone knocked on our door and, when we opened it, a woman came in bringing a small decorated tree. A little later another came, and so we were introduced to a delightful custom. In later years on Christmas Eve each child that I had delivered would bring a little tree with a gift on it: a pair of slippers, a partridge or a pack of cookies. We always had more than one tree; in fact, by the time we left Hopedale after seven years, our living room looked like a tiny forest at Christmas.

Early Easter morning, our first year at Hopedale, I awoke to beautiful music. Hurriedly dressing and going outside, I saw that the music was coming from the church tower. The players stood in a circle, high up in the tower, and played their horns, trumpets and other musical instruments. Each instrument was wrapped in old clothes or skins in an effort to keep them warm enough to play. The men had frost on their hair and faces. As soon as the people heard the music, they all came to church and together we all went to the cemetery. I'll never forget that first Easter service. There was a beautiful, rosy sunrise which glistened on the end of the mouthpieces of the instruments turning them to gold. The white breath of the singers hung in the air with a rosy tint. It was a most impressive ceremony, one which I attended every year we were there.

Other highlights of winter were the days when the mail came. About once every three months the mail arrived. It came all the way along the coast by dog-team. The mailman was a most welcome visitor. He brought news from all along the coast, as well as soiled, battered-looking mailbags. It was very disappointing at times to find that when the mail was opened it contained mostly papers and magazines. Personal letters or packages were often left behind if the load was too heavy. We got used to it and learned to appreciate getting a Christmas gift sometime in August. It was all a part of the life we chose to live.

I have special memories of each season from the years we spent at Hopedale. Spring was a time of lovely sunny days and good dog-team travel in the mornings, when we would go visiting friends in other settlements, stopping to boil up in some sheltered spot on the way. It was the time when you could see seals come up to breathe through holes in the ice, or hear the ice crack and groan as the tides rose and fell. There would be fishing for trout through the cracks of the ice. The days were long and the nights frosty. We always travelled early, before the heat of the sun softened the ice. Each afternoon, when the dogs' travel was over, they would be fed and have their feet attended to so that they could travel the next day. I was used to this kind of life and took some of its pleasures for granted, but always there was Sid, who was enchanted by the newness of each experience and who helped me take the pleasure of a child in all the wonders that the north had to offer.

It was also spring one year that an Eskimo friend of mine passed by my kitchen on her way fishing. I called to her saying I wish I had time to go with her. It was such a lovely afternoon. Later a raging blizzard came on swiftly. Just after supper the men gathered for a search since the woman had not returned. They roped themselves together and started the search. They gave up when the wind got so bad that they could scarcely stand on their feet. Early the next morning they found her on Ellen Island, just a few yards from the mainland. She had crawled into an old packing carton for shelter and died there. It was a sad day for all of Hopedale. Looking back, it seems to me that in those days death was accepted more readily. There were few people with medical training and there was no real way to get a sick person to medical help if it was needed. People lived in a way that lessened the dangers of illness or accident as much as possible, always knowing that, occasionally, being prepared and careful was not enough. In those situations death was accepted.

Late in the spring everybody would be down on the beach painting, mending and readying their boats for the summer. As soon as the ice moved out there would be a big to-do when everybody went to help launch the boats. Women and children sang work songs to the accompanying grunts of the men. At last there would be a splash as the stern hit the water. After launching there was always some boat putt-putting about. The old Acadia engines were slow but most always reliable and easily repaired by people who seemed to have a knack for mechanics.

Summer had its going and coming of boats with supplies and passengers and the excitement of children as they tasted bars and candy after a long winter. A particular favorite summer sight in Hopedale for me was the loading of salt in the salt store for curing fish. This was done by a bucket brigade, made up mostly of women. The bucket brigade seemed to me to be a lot of work and one time I asked Sid if there wasn't an easier way to handle the salt. Sid replied that of course there was: however, another system would mean that the women would not earn the few dollars earmarked for unloading the salt.

Summer was also a time of greeting old friends as the boats went back and forth, and making new friends with people visiting the coast.

Autumn was simply beautiful. Against the stark grayness of the rocks, the brilliant reds of the berry bushes stood out in bold relief. It was a pleasant time to walk in the hills and gather the remaining berries before the snow came. Every day men went after ducks and geese for the winter. Fish were spread on rocks, in sunny weather, to dry for winter eating. Women were busy preparing boots and clothing. The first signs of winter would be scattered snowstorms, then when ice began to form along the edges of the beach, it would be time to pull up the boats. One fall there was a very tragic ending to the "hauling-up" ritual. As we all came back from the beach the dogs made a sudden rush down to the beach and it was noticed that one little girl had been left behind. By the time the men reached the beach, there was nothing left of her.

This was a double tragedy, for the dogs that had killed the little girl were shot. That winter every team in Hopedale was short and it was a difficult time for everybody.

At Hopedale it was almost as if the year would end when the last steamer of the season came and went. We would all go about our last few vital tasks before settling down for the winter. It is true that we sometimes felt that we were isolated in Hopedale (for me this feeling of isolation may have been at its worst when Ma died — I was also unable to get out when Pa died a few years later). But, looking back, the years that I spent in Hopedale were among the happiest of my life. My husband and I spent much time getting to know each other and our love for the land grew. Meanwhile, our children grew up around us.

When the time came for me to have my second baby I wanted to stay at home, as I had done with David. But Sid said, "No. The boats are running and you'll go to Cartwright."

I drove it off until the last minute, leaving Hopedale just a few days before my expected date of delivery. I was only on the boat a few hours when I knew I was in labour. A nurse, who was on the boat travelling out, went to the bridge and informed the captain. Through the speaking tube, he advised the engine room to stoke her up and give her all speed to Cartwright. "Mrs. Loder is going to have her baby."

I was in the hospital one half-hour after arriving when I had my beautiful and beloved little girl, Carlene. I was back in Hopedale when the steamer returned from the south.

I was kept busy with nursing so an Eskimo girl who helped in the house also looked after the children when I was called out.

When David learned to talk, he nearly drove me crazy. He asked constant questions, many of which I couldn't answer, especially since many of his questions were in Inuktituk and German, for his companions were Eskimo children and the children of the missionaries. I often had to ask my Eskimo helper what he was talking about or ask my Dutch friends for translations. He was a real joy though, boy all through and the centre of our lives.

I especially remember how David celebrated the visit of the Governor of Newfoundland to the Labrador coast. As you might imagine, Hopedale didn't get many visitors of this importance. I was asked to sit on the church stage with the official welcoming party and later to serve tea to the visitors. We were days and weeks getting ready for the visit. Decorations were made from spruce boughs. An archway was placed on the wharf. The place was cleaned up and the church was also decorated with boughs, mosses and flowers. Finally everything was in readiness. As one of my final preparations I took David aside and tried to tell him how to behave and what to do. He was to sit with the girl who watched him and later, when we were at tea, he was to stay with her. I told him over and over that he mustn't rush into the room and tell me he wanted to pee the way he always did. I told him if he wanted to pee he was to come into the room and put up his hand and I would know what he meant. David promised he would be good.

The day arrived and we were all in church. Just as I was about to speak a high-pitched little voice piped up, "I can go on the stage. 'Tis my mommy and I can go with my own mommy." I was embarrassed, but the Governor didn't seem to mind. Later, when I was pouring tea, the living room door opened and there was David with his hand held up high. In a clear voice he said, "And my BM too." There was a doctor in the group and he just about choked laughing. I'm not sure that the others ever figured out what the big joke was.

At about the time that David was ready for school Sid was offered a position in St. John's, with the Ministry of Labrador Affairs in the new provincial government. Again I was leaving the land I loved, but we both agreed that Sid's work was important to Labrador and we made our plans to come home again when Sid's work was done. I had come to Hopedale as a new bride and now, seven years later, I was leaving with a family and many wonderful memories of the years.

Our friends gathered on the wharf to see us off and, as the *Kyle* sailed out of the harbour, the little boats circled about as the men played their brass instruments as a gesture of farewell.

The next nineteen years were spent on the island of Newfoundland and were a very important part of my life. However, this book is mainly about Labrador, so I hope my friends in St. John's will forgive me if this part of my life is skimmed over in this book.

In Newfoundland we first went to Harbour Grace, where I met my husband's brother and his family and, in no time, we were all great friends. David was fascinated with all the new things — chickens, horses and cows were his special interests.

Finally we found a house in St. John's and moved to get ready for school. It was a new life and sometimes I felt it was a dangerous one for the children. Cars rushed by on the street a few feet from the door. I spent much of my time training the children how to cross the streets, use traffic lights and so on. Although I have always preferred living in the country, I was glad to be in a city when I discovered how far medicine had advanced during the second World War, while I had been isolated in Hopedale. My children were my first concern. At last they were able to get protection against childhood diseases, were able to be checked by doctors and dentists and were able to go to a good school. For me it was also a forgotten pleasure to have hot and cold water running from taps, and to be able to wash with a machine and not by hand. It gave me much extra time. We joined the church and the PTA and soon I was busy with church and school affairs. But, busy as I was, there was something missing. I longed to be nursing.

It wasn't long before someone whom I knew needed a private nurse and, of course, that was the start. As long as my children were home, I would do private-duty nursing, especially at night. I made up my mind that I would do full-time nursing when my little girl was attending school full time. It was wonderful to be back nursing again, with all the new medical wonders and with expert advice from well-trained doctors and nurses. I began to see how much I had missed and how much I had to learn.

I continued private-duty nursing, becoming gradually familiar with the latest medications and treatments and the practices and procedures of nursing in hospitals. The years went by quickly, and in 1956 I was accepted at the General Hospital as a staff nurse. I worked there happily for the next thirteen years. I developed a great admiration for the

Newfoundland-trained nurses and those who trained them. In my opinion they were second to none.

I felt during those years that I was lucky. I had a wonderful husband, two precious children and I was doing the work that I liked best. We could even afford to have a girl live with us, to be there when the children came home from school, so I had a girl come up from Labrador who lived with us and became one of the family. Oh yes, I was the happiest person ever — then my world shattered.

When I look back I can't remember much about a few years following the death of our daughter. I couldn't accept the tragedy of losing her. She died at the age of ten with a condition known as Guilliam-Barre syndrome. I had always believed in God and prayer. There was no answer in prayer. The church and the minister couldn't help. A psychiatrist couldn't help. There was no relief for the agony and no end to the tears.

I had my work but the happiness and satisfaction was gone. I knew I had to make a change so I asked to be transferred to the pediatric department. I had to take a child in my arms sometimes. I made myself very busy. I loved the children and cuddled them a lot and gradually it eased my pain a little. One day during my lunch break I decided to stay back and cuddle one of the children instead of going down to push food in my mouth, food I didn't want. While I was sitting there the door opened and a doctor came in to make his rounds. He said to me, quite angrily, "Haven't you got anything better to do?" I wanted to tell him he wouldn't be so harsh if he knew what that child was doing for me, but how was he to know we were comforting each other?

Pediatric nursing became my very life. I loved all the children dearly and did all I could for them. It was such a pleasure to see so many of them getting better. There were also difficult times when nothing could be done to save some of them; then all the staff was affected because they cared so much. I worked with the children until the Dr. Charles A. Janeway Children's Hospital was opened, then I elected to stay at the General Hospital. My last job at the General was to set up a volunteer program. It was a pleasure to do this and to watch it grow.

David finished high school, then university, graduating as a mining engineer. My son married, then in 1967 Chris, our grandson, was born and once more we had a baby in and around the house.

Before Chris was a year old, Sid died. Again there were long months of loneliness and difficult adjustments for me.

When David graduated, he got his first posting in Australia. My home became just a house of memories and I felt trapped living there alone. I decided to leave St. John's, so I applied for a position with the Grenfell Mission at North West River, where I had heard that a small pediatric wing was being opened. It seemed that to return to North West River was all that I could ask for. I was going home.

13a. Hopedale. Our apartment is marked with an X.

13b. The arch erected in Hopedale for Governor MacDonald's visit.

CHAPTER EIGHT

Back Home to Stay

I really didn't know what to expect, going back to Labrador after so many years (since leaving Hopedale I had been back in Labrador only twice, visiting family in Rigolet). I knew that there had been great changes. Even as I was in Hopedale, during the 1940s, there had been a major military base built at Goose Bay (in fact my father had piloted boats for the military while the base was being built). There had been major mining operations started at Labrador City and Wabush, where my son had worked briefly. However, it is one thing to read about changes in the newspapers and quite another to go back to the land that I left almost 20 years earlier. I had seen great changes in medicine and in society as a whole while I was in St. John's. What effect might these great changes have had on the places that I knew in my youth?

As I had done in my first tour of duty with the Grenfell Mission, I was expected to go first to St. Anthony for orientation. I could scarcely believe my eyes when I arrived. What a change from the old hospital! A new, very modern, efficient-looking building was not long in operation, staffed by the IGA and named in memory of Dr. Charles S. Curtis.

Once again I found that St. Anthony almost seemed to be in another country. The hospital was staffed, for the most part, by English people and the majority of nurses and some doctors were English. The specialist staff was of excellent calibre and the patients were getting expert care. The old hospital that I had loved so much was all but lost amid the new buildings and had been turned into apartments for staff. When I finally found the building I recognized some parts. I thought of all the good that had been accomplished there by so few people. People like Sir Wilfred Grenfell, Dr. Charles Curtis, Dr. Little and Dr. Paddon all had spent much of their lives in dedicated work for the people of northern Newfoundland and Labrador. I thought how pleased they would have been to see the new hospital. It was to provide such a level of care that they had made their life's work among

111

the people of Newfoundland and Labrador. I was very proud to be numbered once again as a Grenfell Mission worker.

The new hospital was the support base for the many new nursing stations and clinics that had been built in northern Newfoundland and along the Labrador coast while I had been in St. John's. I could sense from the patients I came in contact with that there was, among the people and among the staff as well, a greater feeling of confidence and stability about the quality of health care that was available.

The changes in the care provided were so impressive that I was disappointed to see that some things had not changed. I felt that the medical people continued to ignore many of the opportunities to teach people as we worked with them. Partly as a consequence of this we often failed to learn from them. There has always seemed to be a barrier between medical staff and patients, which still exists today in any health care situation. Patients who return from surgery or treatment often don't understand what they have had done or, if they do ask, are too often told in medical terms which they don't understand. For native people who may be able to speak a little English there are some words for which there is no counterpart in their native tongue. Good interpreters are essential or, better still, native people should be encouraged to train in the medical field. It seems to me that while medical care in the north poses some very real problems, it also provides great opportunities as well.

In St. Anthony there were still some people I had gone to school with, or had met when I worked there. I spent my spare time with them, but I tried not to have too much spare time to fill. I had diagnosed my own condition as one of grief and loneliness, so I worked as hard as I could and it never bothered me if I didn't get off on time. As soon as work was over I would go visiting, then later crawl into bed with a book and fall asleep reading. My pain never entirely went away, despite my busy routine, but I came to accept that life had to go on. It has always helped me during difficult times to feel that I am helping others.

In this manner time passed until the day came, late in November of 1969, when I was posted to proceed to North West River. I could hardly wait to see my family again (for it was here that my brothers Maurice and Bruce and sisters Margaret and Phyllis had settled, along with their families) and to start my new work.

Immediately I was introduced to one of the biggest changes in Labrador life, for in order to get to North West River I had to make my first trip in the Mission plane. I soon found that this would be my favourite method of travel. The Mission was known to have excellent pilots, whose confidence soon put one at rest. I particularly liked the low flying — mountains, bays, and little settlements could be seen clearly on good days. Even after that first trip I felt that I knew the country in a way that I had not before. I was picked up in Goose Bay by the Mission truck from North West River by Jack Watts, the administrator and number-one man at the Grenfell Mission in North West River for many, many years. I had worked under him before I went to the United States to attend school and had been a great admirer of his selflessness, devotion to duty and ability to keep things running smoothly.

As we bumped and slid down the dirt road, through snow, Mr. Watts told me little bits and pieces of news: who was head nurse, how many doctors there were, how the pediatric wing was coming along. While we talked my eyes were taking in the beauty of the Labrador that I loved, especially the Mealy Mountains with their snow-covered peaks, high in the sunny sky. I had almost forgotten the peace and absolute quiet of Labrador. We came up over a little hill and there lay the beautiful community of North West River. It was all so familiar: the Hudson's Bay Company, the hospital, Wood Cottage with the dormer windows, the home of my older sister and, farther along the beach was the point known as Aunt Flo's Point, and houses scattered all up and down along the river.

Mr. Watts introduced me to the head nurse and the rest of the staff. One doctor was from Australia and the doctor in charge was our own Dr. Tony Paddon, now a much experienced doctor, who had been born in Labrador and had taken over his father's work.

Dr. Paddon and his colleague gave of themselves day and night for the patients and the people of Labrador. They kept abreast of new methods, drugs and treatments and helped the nurses keep up to date as well. As I felt when I worked under Dr. Curtis, work was such a pleasure that I would have done my job for nothing. Patients were very much at home in the hospital and they dreaded to have to go to St. Anthony or St. John's for further treatment. They felt the hospital at North West River was their hospital. Interpreters were readily available, but Dr. Paddon had little need for interpreters, for he was a Labradorian, born and bred, and knew the Labrador people extremely well.

My challenge was to develop a good pediatric department in our hospital and I dug in with all my might. The two doctors were the very best and I found the children in our care had the best that could be offered anywhere. I worked long, hard hours and soon we had a pediatric wing that was always full and we felt that we could at last look after the children here, rather than sending them to St. Anthony where they were far away from family and friends. This meant a lot to me, having had to spend so much of my young life away from home.

My days were full. My evenings were spent visiting family and friends and, after some months, I began to feel much more content with my life. Some of the loneliness was gone and if I still had some painful memories, well, I knew that North West River was where I would most likely find peace.

The majority of the children were Indian and Inuit, and what beautiful children they were! Most were used to being much loved at home so they responded beautifully to those who loved them. My life was beginning to seem worthwhile to me once more. I felt I had patients who needed me.

I was often extremely busy, since I was the only professional on pediatrics, doing the medications and injections, but I had the help of the Newfoundland-trained nursing assistants. There was still much tuberculosis in Labrador, particularly among the native people, and treating TB was a great part of my work. Since there was only one RN on evenings and nights, I did as much of the medications and treatments as was possible in the day shift. I loved every minute of my work and eagerly looked forward to each day.

For the first three years that I worked at North West River, I saved every cent I could. In 1971 I started to build a little home for myself and, once I was convinced that I could afford it, I had a great longing to see my son and his family in Australia. The pediatric unit was now stable and well run, so I applied for and obtained a three month leave of absence. I made my bookings. Since this would probably be the only time I would ever see Australia, I decided to see as much of the places along the way as I could, so I included stopovers in Fiji and New Zealand in planning my journey.

I found some things in Australia that reminded me of Labrador, particularly the vastness of the country and the small company plane that took me on the last leg of my journey, to the mining town of Newman, where my son lived with his wife, Roberta, and my grandchildren (my granddaughter, Melynda, was born just before my visit). For the most part, however, Australia was so different from the life that I had been used to that I could not hope to take in everything that I saw and had to content myself with storing up memories, to be considered and cherished in the years to come. I should, however, make a brief mention of the strangest Christmas that I ever spent, in overpowering heat, in the middle of the Australian summer. To think that I left North West River on a cold, snowy November day, dressed in snowboots and all my warm clothes!

For the next three years I lived a very busy, interesting and satisfying life, working on what I had come to think of as "my" pediatric ward. Although the hospital was very small, it was run very efficiently in spite of the difficulties encountered in getting some of the equipment and supplies that were needed. Transportation was difficult between North West River and Goose Bay. A patient who needed to go to St. John's or to Montreal would first have to go to Goose Bay. At that time the only means of getting across the river was by cable car. At times, when the cable car was out of commission, we would have to go on a komatik which was pulled by a snowmobile and go out around the edge of the frozen river ice to the other side and then transfer to a waiting car. Then it was twenty miles or more over a rough dirt road. In winter the road could often be icy and dangerous. Some six or seven years before the completion of the road, it was even worse. Each summer the road would be torn up and sometimes the float plane couldn't land, so a patient would have to be conveyed by small boats across the river to connect with a van. I remember a day when a comatose baby was brought to the hospital. Arrangements were hurriedly made with the Janeway Children's Hospital in St. John's. The baby was placed in an incubator, with a doctor in attendance. I went along to help them get into the cable car and then transfer them to the van on the other side of the river. It was much easier in the van, as the doctor had more room to move. With a sigh of relief I returned to the hospital knowing that the baby was finally on its way. Later, when the driver returned to the hospital, he told us of a harrowing experience. Some distance up the road they encountered a large steel pipe that went right across the road making it impossible to pass. There was no room to turn around. Fortunately a small Volkswagen on the way to North West River came along and the driver quickly grasped the urgency of the situation. With a great deal of difficulty, the doctor and patient were transferred to the little car. It must have been a nightmare for the doctor, who huddled over the baby and managed to keep it alive until they reached the plane in Goose Bay. The baby recovered eventually so it was all worthwhile.

Taking patients who had broken limbs over that bumpy road was always difficult, as it was for women in labour and other seriously ill patients.

The pediatric wing was always full. For years I had been busy carrying around the medication tray that was loaded with tubercular drugs. One day it dawned on me that I was carrying very little for TB patients; most treatments now were for other things: chest infections, ear infections, broken limbs, and quite a few children were there simply for tender loving care, because of turmoil in the home. I really felt good that TB was coming under control. It showed that our efforts to wipe out this dreaded condition were being rewarded. At the same time, it was obvious that family violence was becoming a major problem.

Dr. Paddon had been in touch for some time with government regarding concern for children who were coming into our hospital who really did not need to be there, but who needed a good home somewhere. I'm sure that it was largely due to his intervention that it was finally decided to build such a home for children in North West River.

I had been working now for six years on pediatrics, so I decided, before I got to thinking I was indispensable, it would be good to work at setting up this home. I made it known that when the position was available I would be applying: in the meantime I watched nearly every nail that went into that place. Sometimes I made suggestions to the builders that would make things a little easier for those who would be working there. Sometimes I went to Dr. Paddon with requests, and I always felt encouraged because he listened and intervened with government when necessary. Very often I found myself thinking back to my education at Muddy Bay and St. Anthony. I wanted this home to be the best possible for the children.

By the time it was completed, the staff was selected and I was transferred from the hospital to be supervisor in the Home. I was fortunate in that I was allowed to travel to St. John's to select the curtains and other furnishings. The Home was filled as soon as it opened. It was a busy, happy, beautiful place. Children came from all over the coast and were soon at home with each other. There was a large playroom with plenty of toys for the amusement and education of the children. The staff worked hard to make it a real home and gave much attention to learning from the children about their needs, in order to provide the kind of loving care that was needed. The children participated in the activities of the seasons. Their meals were simple, using their familiar foods. We tried to keep things as much like home as possible, in order that the children who stayed for long periods would be able to integrate back into their family circle with as much ease as possible.

We almost always had a full nursery and most of the newborn babies needed adoption, so whenever the children went out to play I was usually left back with the babies or those who were in need of nursing. Everyone helped. If the children were out during the babies' feeding time, the laundress or cook or cleaning lady would help. This home was exceptionally well placed, in North West River. The hospital was there, so the children could often see their parents or relatives when they came to the hospital. The location was also a fortunate one for adoption purposes. Adoptive parents could fly in to Goose Bay, come to North West River, get their babies and return home on the same day.

I worked happily at the home for two years and was able to see that a good program had been firmly established. By then I was sixty-three years old and was having a few problems with my flat feet. There was no thought in my mind of giving up nursing altogether, so I decided to stay as part-time relief until my retirement was due. It was a tough decision to leave all those wonderful children. I comforted myself by promising to visit them often and, of course, wherever I worked there would be children. For the next two years I worked as a relief nurse at the hospital in North West River or at the nursing stations along the coast. It was a very interesting part of my career.

When we first discussed my plans for part-time nursing, Roberta Clegg, the director of nursing services at that time, said that she would try not to use me too much. Later we both laughed at that statement because she was always needing a relief nurse and I couldn't say no. Roberta became a very dear friend and a great source of support.

For a while my part-time nursing was indeed part time. I relieved nurses who were on holidays, or ill, and most of the time I was working in pediatrics where I was very much at home. There were also times when I went as relief to the coastal communities. Then I was on my own, much as I had been earlier, in Cartwright or Mary's Harbour. I got to know other parts of Labrador, such as Black Tickle and Charlottetown. I also went to Nain one winter, to relieve the head nurse there. Nain had certainly grown in the years since I had last seen it. There were many, many more houses and the population had more than doubled. There was now a hotel, a new store and a new school. Some of the well-known Mission buildings were gone but the little church still stood. The old hospital, now a nursing station, was conveniently located in the centre of the community. Fifteen or twenty years earlier there had been only one nurse stationed there, now there were four. Clinics were held daily and were always full. The public health nurse visited the schools and homes, while the other three nurses looked after the clinic and any in-patients there. There was daily contact with North West River hospital and a good air service was available. Having other nurses to work removed much of the stress that I had felt as a young station nurse. I was quite content to be there. I knew many of the people from former years and was pleased to be able to renew my friendship with the Hettaschs, the missionaries I had lived with during our years at Hopedale. I spent many evenings visiting friends when my day's work was done. I was very pleased to see that customs I had first known at Hopedale were still kept. On Widow's Day, the women invited me to join them in their ceremonies. We attended church services and later in the day were served a delicious meal by the younger married women.

Wherever I went the concern of the people for me was as great as the concern I had for them. I looked after their health as best I could and they looked after my welfare, my travelling in their boats, on their snowmobiles and my living in their homes whenever I made calls through the districts. At times I was only in North West River long enough to wash my clothes or say hello to my family.

Some of the changes that I saw come to Labrador were welcome indeed. I came to love travel by plane and snowmobile (although I was puzzled the first time I had to treat "skidoo knee", a buildup of fluid in the joint caused by kneeling on the seat of a snowmobile). Improvements in communications made the station nurse's job much easier in real emergencies. However, there were other changes that could not be considered advances. One of these was the increase in emergency cases that I saw. In communities where there was a club or hotel there were often brawls resulting in injuries. There was also a disturbing increase in cases such as the one I was confronted with one Sunday morning, about three o'clock, when I was awakened by a loud knocking on the clinic door. I opened the door to see a woman standing before me with blood-splattered clothing and her head was covered with a blood-soaked towel. She had been severely beaten over several days during a drunken spree. Some of her wounds were already infected while others were fresh and needed suturing. I stayed with her all weekend and by then she was strong enough to go home. All such cases were reported to the RCMP, but often the crisis had passed before the authorities could do much.

One time I was asked to go to Rigolet, my old home. There was still no clinic at Rigolet. Staff from North West River made periodic trips there and the Public Health Nurses would go down for a few days to do the immunization programs. General clinics were held at a house in the village. Finally, IGA rented the basement of the school to hold clinics for the doctor and/or dentist and visiting specialists. I was the first nurse to go to Rigolet to spend more than a few days. I was very proud of this. (As far as I know I am still the only registered nurse who was born at Rigolet.) Rigolet had changed a great deal. All the familiar buildings were gone except for a few old HBC houses. The Hudson's Bay house that my family had last lived in still stood, as did the old Customs house and the cooper's shop. The old school I had once attended was now a residence. The wooden walkways that connected the buildings were almost all gone and, in the cove where my father had built a little home for us, there was now a school. It was in this school that the clinic was held and where I would live until freeze-up, when the Mission plane would be able to land on the ice.

Although Rigolet had changed, I did not see many signs of real progress. Soft drink cans and potato chip bags were everywhere. There was a truck or two with only one rough road which went from the school to the tiny old wharf. There were electric lights and telephones, but no water or sewerage system, and the coastal boats still anchored a way off from the shore and all the freight was brought ashore by scows. There was no church but, when the minister came, services were held in the little old school building. The HBC still operated the only store and now people could purchase many more items, including some fresh fruits and meats (although at extremely high prices) and junk food. I was disappointed to find that "progress" in Rigolet had not seemed to make for many real improvements in the quality of life.

If life there was no easier, Rigolet had its attractions still. The people were as friendly and hospitable as during my youth and, of course, many were my relatives. As I looked out over the bay, before me was all the beauty and peace that is Labrador. Within minutes I could go to the bays, coves, heads, hills and mountains, fertile with mosses, green grass, flowers, berries and wildlife: free of tins, paper and disposable diapers. Frequently I thanked God; for allowing me to be born in such a land and for allowing me to return to find peace.

14b. Preparing to leave on a visit.

14a. Indians from Seven Islands visiting the store at Hopedale.

CHAPTER NINE

Epilogue

It was while I was at Black Tickle that I received a call from my supervisor, asking me if I would consider taking over as director of nursing at North West River hospital. For a while I was shocked into silence. With a year and a half to go before my retirement from nursing, my all-time dream was about to come true! I didn't know what to say, because I was content to continue as a relief nurse until retirement. However, after some consideration, I accepted the challenge. The last year and a half of my career was spent as director of nursing at the dear little hospital I had always loved.

Would you believe that, after all my childhood dreams, I found that being a director of nursing wasn't what I wanted after all? It did, however, give me considerable satisfaction to realize that, despite my life's ambition, I had really been living my dream all along, as a bedside nurse. I had come to cherish the people and the close contact that bedside nursing gives. Being a director of nursing often meant that I sat in an office making out forms, conducting interviews, dealing with correspondence and other duties that took me away from the patients' bedsides. I did thoroughly enjoy my year and a half as director and, although I may not have been the best of administrators, I kept close contact with staff and patients. As my retirement drew near, I wondered what I would do with all the free time that would be available. I could have stayed on longer, but I felt I needed a long rest, and perhaps I could find something to occupy my time later. On the eve of my retirement, the hospital staff gave me a lovely farewell. There was a banquet with speeches and gifts, and my relatives and friends were all present. I think I was the proudest person in the world when it was announced at the banquet that I would receive an honourary degree in the spring from Memorial University of Newfoundland for the work I had done for the people of Labrador. Many nurses had done the same work as I had, but I was pleased to accept this honour, as I felt it would serve as a tribute to all the nurses that worked with the Grenfell Mission. That same fall I attended the annual meeting of the Association of Registered Nurses of Newfoundland to have conferred upon me an honourary life membership. I felt that this honour from the members of my own profession was the highlight of my career.

During my retirement I found, happily, that there were many ways that I could still be of service. I became a member of the community council at North West River and had time to work among senior citizens, with the church and with other community organizations. I also served on the board of the Grenfell Regional Health Service. There I found an audience for some of my theories about the opportunities for educating the people that should be a part of any health service. I also tried to encourage recognition of the contribution made to Newfoundland and Labrador by the "loyal soldiers" of the Grenfell Mission — such people as Jack Watts and Selma Carlson.

As I look back on my life's work, I find that I can allow myself some satisfaction. I had a childhood dream that never changed. I willingly endured the waiting, the deprivation of home and family, the long years of study and the years of homesickness to obtain my goal. All seemed like nothing against the satisfaction of accomplishing the task that I had set for myself. As Ma always told us, "Anything worthwhile is worth working for".

There can be no doubt in my mind that my years of nursing were worthwhile. I am constantly reminded of the worth of my chosen career. On the occasion when the first Inuit magistrate was installed many Labradorians were delighted. There can have been few more delighted than I: he was one of the babies I delivered in Hopedale. There have also been countless occasions when I have met a former patient, like the young man whom I treated for a jigger wound one day at Charlottetown. I sewed him up, gave him antibiotics and told him when to take the sutures out, a routine procedure. Some years later, when I was travelling somewhere a man came up to me, all smiles. "You don't remember me," he said, holding out his hand, slightly scarred, but obviously a hand that he could still use for fishing, hunting or trapping — in short, a hand that could provide for his family. "You did this for me."

15a. Sid getting ready to leave on a business trip

15b. Myself and some patients at Hopedale.

16. Sid and I our first year at Hopedale.